John Rowland West

A short elementary treatise on the Holy Eucharist

John Rowland West

A short elementary treatise on the Holy Eucharist

ISBN/EAN: 9783742836816

Manufactured in Europe, USA, Canada, Australia, Japa

Cover: Foto ©Lupo / pixelio.de

Manufactured and distributed by brebook publishing software (www.brebook.com)

John Rowland West

A short elementary treatise on the Holy Eucharist

A SHORT ELEMENTARY TREATISE

ON

The Holy Eucharist.

BY THE

REV. J. R. WEST, M.A.,

VICAR OF WRAWBY.

"Sacraments are the powerful Instruments of GOD to Eternal Life."
—*Hooker.*
"As it was at first, so it hath been ever since. CHRIST came into the world, and the world knew Him not. So CHRIST hath remained in the world, by the Communication of this Sacrament, and yet He is not rightly understood, and less truly valued."—*Bishop Jeremy Taylor.*
"We should aspire to know the hidden rich things of GOD, that are wrapped up in His Ordinances."—*Archbishop Leighton.*

LONDON:
JOSEPH MASTERS, ALDERSGATE STREET,
AND NEW BOND STREET.
NEW YORK: POTT AND AMERY.
MDCCCLXVIII.

PREFACE.

As Dr. Waterland has well said, "Subjects which have already passed through many hands, and which have been thoroughly sifted and considered by the ablest and best heads, in a course of eighteen hundred years, leave room rather for judgment than for invention; for little new can now be thought of that is worth notice, and it is much wiser and safer to take the most valuable observations of men most eminent in their several ways, than to advance poor things of our own, which perhaps are scarce worth the mentioning in comparison."

The writer of the following pages does not, therefore, pretend to advance "*poor things of his own invention;*" he lays little claim to originality. He has rather endeavoured to collect together, in a convenient form, that which has been thought and written before by great and learned men. He has not, however, considered it suitable to the object of this book to cite many authorities or to quote many passages from learned authors; for this book is intended, not for those who have leisure and opportunity to refer to such learned authors, but rather for ordinary Christians, who may need such help as is here offered them; so that the explanations and doctrines here set forth are not offered on the authority of this or that learned man, but they are rather set forth on their own merits, and the Holy Scriptures are the only authority continually appealed to.

CONTENTS.

	PAGE
Introduction	1
This Sacrament a Trial of Faith	3
The Divine Author	6
The Command	7
The Time of the Institution	8
The Weakness of the First Communicants	10
The Tree of Life	11
The Manna	15
The Revelation given to S. Paul	18
The Propriety of the Outward Elements	19
The Use of the Outward Elements	22
The Divine Presence hidden under lowly Signs	28
Worship by Sacrifice	31
The Priesthood after the Order of Melchisedec	39
The Passover	44
Our LORD's Actions and Words at the Institution	50
The Spiritual Sense	67
The One only Sacrifice once offered	70
On the Words "Spiritual," "Substance," and "Mystery."	79
The Real Presence	84
Transubstantiation	91
S. John vi. 48—59	94
The Similarity of the Manner of our LORD's Teaching in the case of both the Sacraments	99
S. Paul's Commentaries	103
The Benefit	105
The Quickening Flesh of the Second Adam	113
The Application of the Atonement	118

	PAGE
The Eucharistic Sacrifice	122
The Suitableness of this Service to our Wants	131
The Necessity	132
The Frequency of Celebration	135
The Christian Altar	140
The Sacrament of Christian Unity	145
The External Ritual	154
Notes	163

PRAYER.

The earth, O LORD, is full of Thy mercy; O teach me Thy statutes.

Thy hands have made me and fashioned me; O give me understanding, that I may learn Thy commandments.

Open Thou mine eyes; that I may see the wondrous things of Thy law.

O send out Thy light and Thy truth; that they may lead me, and bring me unto Thy holy hill and to Thy dwelling;

And that I may go unto the Altar of GOD, even unto the GOD of my joy and gladness.

A SHORT ELEMENTARY TREATISE ON THE HOLY EUCHARIST.

INTRODUCTION.

"What mean ye by this Service?"   (Exod. xii. 26.)

IF a man does not endeavour to understand the meaning of the chief Rite of the Religion which he professes, how can he be in earnest in the matter of Religion at all? What would have been thought of a Jew who did not understand the meaning of the Passover? And what must be said of a Christian who does not understand the meaning of the Holy Eucharist?

The very poor and insufficient notion which many entertain concerning this Divine Institution is indeed painful. The best notion they seem to have of it is, that it is a solemn way of remembering the Death of the SAVIOUR of the World, by eating a little Bread and drinking a little Wine! Just as if to *eat bread and drink wine* were an appropriate way, simply, of remembering a Person's Death. If, indeed, that were *all*, surely we might put ourselves in remembrance of our SAVIOUR's Death, one might think, in a much more impressive manner, by reading the Sacred Narratives of that Death.

Besides, to think that this act of remembrance on our part is *all* that is meant, is quite to put aside one half of the Words of Institution. "*This do, in remembrance of Me,*" seems to be all that is thought of: the other words, "*This is My Body, This is My Blood,*" are overlooked and forgotten, or explained away.

Ignorance, indeed, is no bar to our receiving Grace, where that ignorance is not careless and wilful but unavoidable and excusable. All cannot attain unto the same degrees of knowledge; but all may attain unto some degrees, and all ought to give the best care and diligence they can to understand the meaning of the chief Rite of their Religion. Whatever else a Christian may be lawfully ignorant of, of this he may not. Here the precept is very binding upon all, "*Add to your Faith, Knowledge.*"

If in the very least of the Works of GOD there are many uses and properties, there surely must be very great and high ones indeed in this Holy Institution; into which we should earnestly desire to look, as far as is revealed to us. For this is the One only Service ordained by the LORD Himself for His whole Church even till He come again. This is the very and only Centre of Worship for the whole Christian Dispensation: the one common Act of Worship for all Christendom.

How, therefore, can any Christian be a properly instructed Christian, who has not learnt to understand in some degree his chief Act of Worship?

If the ancient Passover was in every part of it full of meaning, how much more so must be this Holy Eucharist, of which that ancient Rite was only a type and shadow and forerunner?

If, then, the following pages shall be found at all useful in helping any to form more adequate and proper notions concerning the nature of the chief Service of the Christian Religion, the writer will be indeed most thankful to the Giver of all good.

THIS SACRAMENT A TRIAL OF FAITH.

"From that time many of His disciples went back, and walked no more with Him." (S. John vi. 66.)

Manifold is the trying of our faith in GOD. Even in our commonest duties there is some degree of this trial awaiting us every day; and sometimes GOD orders for us very special trials of our faith in Him. In different ages of the Church there may be different kinds of trials, and in different nations. In those days when the LORD Himself was present among men here below, in a condition of great humiliation and weakness, there was a very special trial for those around Him, whether they would believe in Him or not. Many failed to perceive His hidden Deity; they knew Him not, their very Maker, although He gave them signs and proofs enough.

And now we may truly say, that, just as that Presence of the LORD Himself was the occasion of a very special trial for all those who were then around Him, so the Presence of His Kingdom amongst ourselves is the occasion of a very special trial to us now. That new Kingdom of Heaven, of which the holy Baptist gave plain warning as being close at hand in his day, is now come, and is now in the midst of us, with all its infinite Mysteries; but its Presence is not yet perceived by any signs of visible Power or of outward Glory. On our LORD's Ascension, in our nature, into the Presence of the FATHER, His New Kingdom began in Heaven above; and on the Day of Pentecost it came down to this world also, by the Coming of the HOLY GHOST. Then the Ministration of the Spirit began, and the New Kingdom of Heaven was opened upon earth to all believers; and we, at our Baptism, entered into it, and we are now living in it. We are even now come unto the Heavenly Jerusalem. (Heb. xii. 22.)

But this New Kingdom of GOD Incarnate, with all

its Heavenly Mysteries, is as yet amongst us without observation of sight or sense; it is as yet an object of faith only. It is, therefore, quite possible that we may fail to perceive its presence. Here there is a *very* special *trial of faith* for all of us. And so, in the end, when this trial-time is past by and gone, one grievous mark, which will mark for ever too many of us, will be this: "*As for the Mysteries of God, they knew them not.*" (Wisdom ii. 22.)

Here we may consider, that, if there were no Mysteries in the Christian Revelation, it would be a great reason for not receiving it as Divine; because all the works of GOD are and must be so very far beyond the reach of our present knowledge. When we search into any of the works of GOD in the kingdom of nature, we are soon baffled with amazing wonders on all sides. Not one seed, not one bud, not one insect is there, which does not contain something far beyond all our present knowledge.

And shall we find nothing but what is easy and simple, when we search into the greater and higher works of GOD in the Kingdom of Grace? Surely we must expect to find here the most stupendous and glorious of all the Mysteries of GOD.

And amongst all these infinite Mysteries of the New Kingdom of CHRIST, the Holy Eucharist is doubtless one of the greatest, coming next in order, perhaps we may say, to the Mystery of the Divine Incarnation itself. So that, from the very first, there has ever been a very special trial of faith in connection with the Holy Eucharist.

When our LORD Himself, in the synagogue at Capernaum, prepared the disciples for the institution of the Holy Eucharist, by discoursing upon the infinite Gifts conveyed to us in it, many of them could not tell how to believe His words. The very first revelation of this great Mystery of the Kingdom of Heaven, we see, offended many; even such as had not humble and teachable hearts. They said at once,

"*This is a hard saying: who can hear it?*" And so, "*from that time, many of His disciples went back, and walked no more with Him.*" Their faith was not strong enough to bear the trial.

There is the very same trial for us also. The revelation of any one of the Mysteries of CHRIST becomes at once, of necessity, a special trial for us, whether we will receive and believe it, or not. And the heavenly mystery contained in the Holy Eucharist is so exceedingly great, that it has ever been, all along, one of the most special trials of faith. From the first revelation of it, in that synagogue at Capernaum, even down to the present day, the faith of many disciples has been too weak to receive the tremendous saying of the LORD, "*This is My Body.*"

Let us therefore pray for humble and teachable hearts, so that we may not be of those who are offended at this saying; but that it may be "*given unto us to know this Mystery of the Kingdom of Heaven,*" (S. Matth. xiii. 11,) for of our own selves we cannot rightly receive it. And let us bear in mind that, when we *have* learnt anything, we are nevertheless still only just beginning to learn; for, "*If any man think that he knoweth anything, he knoweth nothing yet, as he ought to know.*" For who of us can search perfectly into any one of the works of Infinite Wisdom?

Let us, then, not be of those disciples who draw back in unbelief, and refuse to learn, when the Mystery of the Holy Eucharist is openly set before them. When some heavenly truth is proposed to our faith, let us not be offended because there is something in it which reaches far beyond the narrow limits of our human capacity. Let us not be offended, neither at the seeming weakness of the outward earthly appearance of the Holy Mystery, nor yet at the infinite greatness of the inward Heavenly Grace which lies hidden in it.

THE DIVINE AUTHOR.

In the institution of this Holy Sacrament, let us first remark *Who it is that instituted it.*

It is no prince or king of this world; it is no angel or archangel of heaven; but it is even GOD Himself, manifest in the flesh, Who ordains this Holy Sacrament. It is instituted by Him, than Whom none is greater, none higher, none more glorious; even by the very LORD Himself, in His own Person, with His own Hands, and with His own Words. It is a Holy Service, appointed and set in order for us all by the Divine Head of the Church Himself. He who made all the worlds; He who said, "*Let there be Light, and there was Light;*" He who placed the Tree of Life in the midst of Paradise; even He has now placed this Sacrament in the midst of His Church.

None, indeed, but GOD could institute a Sacrament. It is entirely beyond the power of man. Man might as well try to place a star in the sky as a Sacrament in the Church of GOD. How great, then, *must be* the dignity, and the authority, and the blessing of this Holy Sacrament, which has even GOD Himself for its Author.

Even human institutions may be justly esteemed and contended for, when they are wisely ordered for the benefit of society; but how much more so, the Holy Sacraments of the Gospel, the Institutions of the LORD Himself, instruments in His Hands of heavenly grace and spiritual benefit to all His whole Church to the end of the world.

If all the Works of GOD contain in them some marks of His Power, Wisdom, and Goodness, even all His Works in the lower kingdom of nature, how much more full of His Glory must be His Works in the higher kingdom of Grace? Shall we reverently consider and devoutly admire the wonderful Works of GOD in nature, even in the least plant that grows and in the least insect that breathes, and not *much more* consider and reverence the glories of His Divine Grace in the Mysteries of the Kingdom of CHRIST?

If the Jews so highly and so justly valued their holy Ordinances, because they were of Moses, who was sent by GOD, how much more should we value ours, which have been instituted for us by the immediate hand of GOD our SAVIOUR Himself. If the Institutions of the Jewish Church were glorious, "*how much more*" do the Institutions of the Christian Church "*exceed in glory. If that which is done away was glorious, much more that which remaineth is glorious.*" (2 Cor. iii. 7—11.)

Let us, then, as long as we live, ever give some of our best attention and most reverent consideration to this Divine Institution, this Christian Sacrament, this most Holy Service, instituted for His whole Church by the very LORD Himself, enjoined upon us all by GOD Himself manifest in the flesh.

THE COMMAND.

"*This do. Take, eat. Drink ye all of this.*"

No Command can be more plain or express than this is. "*Remember the Sabbath day, to keep it holy,*" is indeed a very plain and express Command of GOD; but surely not *more* plain or express than this is. There is the very same Divine authority in one as in the other. Have we any right to pick and choose, so to speak, among the Commandments of GOD? May we keep one, and not the other, and yet be safe? Shall we be concerned to observe the Ten Commandments given upon Mount Sinai, and not be concerned to observe this Commandment given by the same LORD GOD at Jerusalem? And ought not the notable circumstance that the LORD Himself lays this Commandment upon us all *with His dying breath* to weigh very powerfully upon our hearts?

What is the best test and safest proof of the reality and of the sincerity of our faith in the LORD JESUS?

Our LORD Himself gives it to us, saying, "*If ye love Me, keep My Commandments.*" Shall we then pretend that we love our SAVIOUR in sincerity and in truth, if we do not keep His Commandments? And again our LORD declares, "*He that hath My Commandments and keepeth them, he it is that loveth Me.*" Shall we then pretend that we love our SAVIOUR, if we do not keep His last great Commandment? Surely we must be grievously deceiving our own selves, if we are unwilling to apply this plain test to our own selves?

But how thankful we should be that our SAVIOUR has made it so plainly *our duty* to come to this Holy Sacrament. Else we might be easily tempted to shrink back from it, on the plea that it is too great, too holy, too Divine a Communion for us. Those fears are silenced by the plain Commandment, "*This do.*" It *is* indeed an infinitely great and holy thing to do; but the LORD Himself, Who knows better than we do what it is, *commands* us. This, therefore, greatly helps us. It is one of our very plainest *duties*. Not to "*do this,*" is to disobey and break a most clear Commandment of GOD; and who that lives in the known and wilful transgression of any one of the Commandments of the LORD can be walking in the path that leadeth unto Life? "*Then shall I not be ashamed, when I have respect unto all Thy Commandments.*"

THE TIME OF THE INSTITUTION.

"*The same night in which He was betrayed.*" (1 Cor. xi. 23.)

Our LORD prepared the minds of His disciples, in some measure, for the Institution of this Holy Sacrament, by His discourse concerning the Holy Communion of His Body and Blood in the synagogue at Capernaum. (S. John vi. 30—59.) For we could hardly anyhow believe that our LORD would have given them this Holy Communion, without having prepared their minds for it beforehand in some measure.

But the actual Institution of this Sacrament our LORD reserved for the most solemn and appropriate time; our LORD reserved it *to His last hour*, the hour before His last sufferings began. He made the actual Institution of the Eucharist to be His last action for us before He entered into His Passion. It was His dying Command, His last Act of Love towards us, before He endured the Cross. The LORD JESUS instituted this Holy Service for us, we may even say, with His dying breath.

And most surely this was not done by any chance. None of our LORD's words, and none of His actions, were apart from His Eternal Wisdom. He foreknew, He chose of set purpose, this time for this Holy Institution. He placed this Sacrament as close as possible to His Cross. As He ordained the Sacrament of Baptism, just as He was about to ascend, so He ordained the Sacrament of His Body and Blood, just as He was about to die. This time was the fittest and the best, most full of deep meaning and intention of Divine Wisdom. Not one action of our LORD's life on earth was there, but had its proper time. This was then made His last action; this is His dying Command: He enjoins this upon us all, even with His dying breath.

Shall we then regard, most carefully and most affectionately, the dying request of any beloved fellow-creature, and not much more regard this dying injunction of our Loving SAVIOUR, Who, as He lays down His life for our sins, institutes and commands this Holy Sacrament? Can we indeed love our only LORD and SAVIOUR, in sincerity and in truth, and not most affectionately and most carefully observe and keep this His last Commandment all our life long; and *then*, most specially of all times, when the time of our own death is close at hand.

THE WEAKNESS OF THE FIRST COMMUNICANTS.

"*This night, before the cock crow, thou shalt deny Me thrice.*"
(S. Matth. xxvi. 34.)

Many say, when they are bidden to the Holy Communion of the Body and Blood of CHRIST, some such words as these: "*I must first become better; I fear I shall fall into sin after it, and that will be worse than if I had not come; I must wait, till I am a stronger Christian.*" But is not this very much the same as if a sick man should say, "*I must wait till I am better, before I take this medicine which the physician has ordered me.*" If indeed any one is indulging in any known and wilful sin, and does not mean to fight against it and to mortify it, then of course he is not fit to partake of this Divine Communion;—but surely it is not mere human weakness that ought to keep us back from it: it is not the fear that we may fall again into sin, which ought to keep us away from this Sacrament. Only consider the case of the first Communicants. Was not their faith in the LORD then very weak? Did they not all, that very night, forsake their LORD and fly from Him? Did not S. Peter himself fall into sin, that very night, very grievously? And yet foreknowing all this, the LORD Himself gave them all the Holy Communion of His Body and Blood. Let us therefore remember that our merciful SAVIOUR has instituted this Sacrament, not for the righteous, but for sinners; not for the holy Angels who never once have sinned, but for us guilty miserable sinners; not for those who never more will sin, but even for such as may after that Reception of His Body and Blood again fall into sin, if they do not watch and pray. This

Holy Sacrament is for us sinners, even for such as do truly repent and believe; not merely for such as are made perfect and strong in repentance and faith; but even for very imperfect and weak beginners; even for those who have as yet but a little and weak faith, if they do indeed in their hearts desire to follow the LORD in the way of Life and to grow in Grace.

Nor, again, is imperfection of *knowledge* a bar to our receiving the heavenly gifts of this Sacrament, if that imperfection be not careless and wilful. The first Communicants were very imperfect in knowledge, until the HOLY GHOST came; but our LORD did not refuse them, because of that imperfection. GOD indeed is surely more pleased with an intelligent and an understanding worshipper than with a mere blind and ignorant faith; but in cases where there is no opportunity of removing that ignorance, it may be entirely pardoned, and the worshipper most graciously accepted.

THE TREE OF LIFE.

Genesis ii. 9.

In preparing our minds to consider the nature of any part of the Christian Revelation, it is very often very advantageous to consider such ancient types and institutions as GOD had been pleased to ordain in former ages to be means of preparing the world for the more perfect institutions and the higher revelations of this last dispensation.

Because the past as well as the present has been the creation of One and the same Divine Mind. The former Dispensations were all so ordered as to be in manifold ways preparatory to this later one, they were all so disposed by the Divine foreknowledge as to be very significant of the Mysteries of CHRIST. Just as S. Paul teaches us, when, having quoted the original sentence spoken to our first parents, "*They two shall* be one flesh;" he writes, "*This is a great mystery: but I speak concerning Christ and the Church:*" for the formation of Eve out of Adam, and the oneness of Adam and Eve, were in the very beginning, types and shadows of the great mysteries of CHRIST and His Church.

So also Paradise was a type of the Church of CHRIST; and its two peculiar Trees were types of the two Sacraments which CHRIST has now placed in His Church.

Let us consider the Tree of Life in the midst of Paradise, which is so remarkable an emblem and shadow of that Sacrament of Life which GOD has now ordained in the midst of the Church.

GOD planted the Tree of Life, not in the open world, but in the garden of Eden, in that sacred enclosure in which was manifested to our first parents the special Presence of GOD. In like manner, GOD our SAVIOUR has now instituted the Sacrament of Life, not in the world at large, but in His Church, of which Paradise was so remarkable a type. No one out of the Church can either administer or receive this Holy Sacrament, but first they must be baptised into the Church of CHRIST.

Other trees had the power given them by GOD of sustaining man's life for some short time, just as they have now. But the Tree of Life had the greater power given it of sustaining man's life from all decay and death for ever. So long as our first parents ate of the fruit of this Tree, they would live for ever, as it is written in the third chapter: "*And now, lest he put forth his hand, and take also of the Tree of Life, and eat, and live for ever.*"

This power of sustaining Life was not indeed in the Tree itself, except as it came from GOD. Because the power of Life, and the power of sustaining Life, must be in GOD alone, and can come from Him alone.

Moreover, we may say, GOD was able, if He had so pleased, to sustain the life of our first parents in immortality, without the use of the fruit of that Tree. But such was not His Will. For several great reasons, GOD made their immortal Life to depend upon their continually partaking of that Tree of Life.

Now we can easily see that this was something very like a Sacrament to our first parents. There was first the outward and visible part or sign, the natural substance, the Fruit of that Tree; which indeed had no power or virtue of its own to preserve man's life for ever. But, then, there was as well the inward invisible part of the Sacrament, the gift coming from GOD, the sustenance of the power of immortal Life, conveyed to our first parents by that appointed means, through that particular channel.

It was not their Innocency which gave our first parents the power of immortal Life. It was not their Faith in GOD which gave them Life or preserved it in them. The power of Life is of GOD alone; it is a distinct Gift of GOD, most precious and amazing indeed. And it was preserved in our first parents, by GOD's appointment, by their continually eating of that Tree of Life.

This plainly foreshadowed something greater than itself. It was a Type, ordered by the foreknowledge of GOD, so as to prefigure that great Sacrament which CHRIST has now placed in the midst of His Church in these last days; in which we receive *the very Food of Immortality*, both for our body and for our soul; for our LORD has said: "*Whoso eateth My Flesh, and drinketh My Blood, hath Eternal Life, and I will raise him up at the last day.*"

It is not for any one of us to say, "*God is able to save me, and to give me eternal Life, without my receiving the Sacrament.*" Adam and Eve might just as well have said in Paradise, "*God is able to support our Life, without our eating of this Tree.*"

Here is an appointed Means of Life for us to use continually. Here is an appointed trying of our humility, and of our obedience, and of our faith, from time to time. And it is also meant to make us feel and know, very plainly, that Life is not our own; that the power of Life is of GOD alone, that is, it comes to us directly from GOD; and that we must seek for its continual preservation and sustenance within us, in that way which GOD is pleased to institute and command.

Our Eternal Life is in CHRIST our New Divine Head; it is communicated to us from Him; it comes to us through our Union with Him. It does not come from our Innocence, nor from our Repentance, nor from our Faith, but simply and only from our Life-giving Head Himself, the Second Adam, GOD the SON Incarnate; and we derive it from Him by the means which He has appointed; in the proper use of which He has promised to bestow the Gift upon us.

For now the true Tree of Life is restored to us, in the midst of the Church of CHRIST. For in the holy Eucharist, which the LORD has commanded to be received by us all, there is the Holy Communion of the Body and Blood of CHRIST, of which Divine Gifts our LORD has said, "*My Flesh is Meat indeed, and My Blood is drink indeed.*"

For as surely as we there receive *the outward and visible part* of the Sacrament, so surely will GOD give us *the inward and invisible part*, which is nothing less than the Living and Life-giving Body and Blood of CHRIST Himself, which is the very spiritual Food and Sustenance of our immortal Life.

In this holy Sacrament therefore we see the fulfilment of the ancient Type; for herein we have access to the true Tree of Life, even to Him Who is our Life. By this Holy Communion we are fed with the very Food of Immortality.

THE MANNA.

"*He gave them food from Heaven.*" (Ps. lxxviii. 25.)

We have most express authority for considering the Manna, with which GOD fed His people for forty years in the wilderness, as a Type or Figure of that heavenly Food which is now given to us in the Sacrament of the Body and Blood of CHRIST. For S. Paul declares to us (1 Cor. x. 11,) that all the events of the journey of the Israelites between Egypt and Canaan, "*happened unto them for ensamples,*" that is, for Types. And referring to the Miracle of the Manna, he says, "*They did all eat the same spiritual Meat.*" S. Paul calls the Manna "*spiritual Meat,*" because of its miraculous nature, as given from heaven; and also on account of its typical nature and spiritual signification, foreshadowing the true Manna, the Spiritual Meat indeed, which is given unto us in the Church of CHRIST, from the Heaven of heavens.

And also our LORD Himself, in His discourse with the Jews at Capernaum, distinctly compares His Gift to us in this Sacrament with the Gift of the Manna to the Israelites in the wilderness. The Jews said: "*What Sign showest Thou, that we may see, and believe Thee? what dost Thou work? Our fathers did eat Manna in the wilderness, as it is written, He gave them bread from Heaven.*" As much as to say, "*That was the wonderful Sign that Moses gave: that was the great Work that God did by him, to prove that He sent him: what Sign showest Thou? what dost Thou work?*" Then our LORD proceeded to discourse on the great Gift that He would give; in comparison with which the gift of the Manna by Moses was nothing at all. He said, "*Moses gave you not that Bread from Heaven; but My Father giveth you the true Bread from Heaven.*" That is to say, That Manna did not really come down from Heaven itself, but only from the clouds; but the True Bread of GOD comes down from Heaven itself. And then our LORD explained what He meant by "*the True Bread,*" the True Manna from Heaven itself: "*The Bread that I will give, is My Flesh, which I will give for the Life of the world.*"

And then He also compared the effect of the Manna given to those Israelites with the effect of the true Manna now given to us, saying, "*Your fathers did eat Manna in the wilderness, and are dead; This is the Bread which cometh down from Heaven, that a man may eat thereof, and not die. Whoso eateth My Flesh and drinketh My Blood hath eternal Life, and I will raise him up at the last day.*" That Manna supported only their bodily life; this true Bread of Heaven supports our eternal Life.

And shortly afterwards our LORD instituted this Sacrament to be the means or channel by which He gives us this true Manna from Heaven itself; for here He says to us, and here only, "*Take, eat; this is My Body;*" at the same time making good His own words, giving us the very Bread of Life.

The great likeness between the ancient Type and the present Antitype will appear more plainly, if we consider its several chief particulars.

I. The Manna was the Food which GOD gave His people for their journey through the wilderness. There was no bread for them in the rocky desert; so GOD supplied them with this food all their journey through. Even so for us in this world there is no support or food for our souls. So GOD gives us the True Bread of Life from Heaven. Our LORD spreads a Table before us, even here in the wilderness, and says to us, "*Take, eat; This is My Body.*" This is "*Meat indeed,*" sufficient to sustain the Life of our souls, all our journey through, even till we come to the true Canaan.

II. Next, the supply of Manna was *a standing Miracle*, a continual Work of GOD, for all those forty years. Even so GOD sends us now the True Manna, from the Heaven of Heavens, by a continual Miracle indeed. This is now our standing Miracle. As soon as the words are said, at the Consecration, "*This is My Body*," then there is present, by the Power of the Holy Spirit, verily and indeed, the Body of CHRIST, to be given to us for our true Spiritual Food and Sustenance, as we journey through the wilderness.

III. Then, let us mark, that when the Israelites saw the Manna, they marvelled; for neither they nor their fathers had ever seen such food; and they called it, "*Manna,*" which word means, "*What is it?*" Even so, we acknowledge and confess that there is an infinite Mystery in the Heavenly Food sent to us from GOD in this holy Sacrament. Who can explain what it is? who pretends to know? We humbly call it the True Manna, saying, "*What is it?*" It quite transcends all our human knowledge.

IV. Again; observe that the Manna fell only in the Camp of Israel. Even so, this holy Sacrament of the LORD's Body is ordained only in the Church.

V. Then also mark, that unless the Israelites partook of this Manna, there was no other Bread for them. Their life could be preserved only by means of this miraculous food. Even so, our Life cannot be supported and preserved unto the glories of the true Canaan, except we partake of the LORD's Body.

VI. But many of these Israelites grew tired of the food which GOD gave them; they loathed it, and called it, in contempt, that "*light Bread;*" and they wished for the more stimulating food of Egypt again. Even so with many Christians, they think little of the true and real Manna, which GOD offers them in this Sacrament, but they prefer something more exciting to the senses, something more new. As for most, in every parish, they do in reality say, by their continual neglect, "*The Table of the Lord is contemptible.*" They fancy they can reach Heaven without this holy Sacrament of the Body of CHRIST. They turn away from it all their life long. Thus they despise the real and great Gifts of GOD; deceiving their own souls with a vain and false religion of mere feeling and excitement.

VII. Many, however, who partook of the Manna fell in the wilderness and never entered into Canaan. Even so, many, it is to be feared, who come to this most Holy Communion, fail to reach Heaven; because they receive It without true repentance and faith, and therefore not unto Life, but unto condemnation.

VIII. Once more; the Manna was sweet to the taste. Even so, to the true Christian, who comes to the Holy Communion of the Body of CHRIST in earnest repentance and with a lively faith, there is here the foretaste of the very sweetness of Heaven itself. For by this Holy Communion, his union with CHRIST is preserved and strengthened; and what can be wanting to the real peace and comfort and joy of that soul which possesses Him Who is the Joy of all Angels, the Glory of all Heaven? Here is the hidden Manna, the Food of Immortality, the very Sweetness of Heaven.

THE REVELATION GIVEN TO S. PAUL.

The History of the Institution of the Holy Eucharist is given us by three of the Evangelists. S. Paul was not present at the Institution, not then being a Disciple of the LORD. But as he was to be so great an Instrument in the hand of the LORD for extending His Church upon earth, a special Revelation was granted him concerning this Divine Institution. The account which this Apostle gives, he takes particular pains to declare he had not received from any of the other Apostles, nor indeed from any man, but even from the LORD Himself. For he writes to the Corinthians, "*For I have received of the Lord that which also I delivered unto you, That the Lord Jesus, the same night, &c.*" (1 Cor. xi. 23.)

And some years before, He took particular pains to declare to the Galatians, that the Gospel which he preached was not derived from any human source, but by immediate Revelation; for he writes, "*I neither received it of man, neither was I taught it, but by the Revelation of Jesus Christ.*"

So that we see that S. Paul had special Revelations granted him, not only as to the truth of the Gospel, but as well also as to the Institution of the Holy Eucharist.

And the account of this Institution as thus received by S. Paul and delivered unto us agrees most exactly, in the history of all our LORD then did and said, with the accounts given by the Evangelists.

Now this surely must impress us with a very deep sense of the importance of this Holy Institution, and must add very great weight to every Action and to every Word used by our LORD at the Institution, when we consider that after His Ascension He thought it needful for the Church that He should thus directly reveal them every one to the Apostle S. Paul; in order that the great Apostle of the Gentiles might have the most perfect knowledge and the most certain confidence concerning this distinctive Rite of the Christian Revelation.

Can anything serve to impress us with a stronger and deeper conviction that this Holy Sacrament is one of those things which our LORD has made to be necessary to our Salvation, more than this single circumstance does?

THE PROPRIETY OF THE OUTWARD ELEMENTS.

As He Who instituted this Sacrament is Himself GOD, all Whose works are done in perfection of Wisdom, we cannot but believe that everything concerning this great Institution is ordered in excellence of knowledge; even the outward and earthly parts of this Sacrament have not been selected and appointed without due suitableness and significance. As our LORD chose Water for the outward part, the visible sign, of Baptism, with great significance, even so we may observe great meaning and propriety in the choice of Bread and Wine to be the outward parts of this Sacrament; for these outward Elements are very significant, *first*, of the Sacrifice of the LORD's Death, the Bruising of the Great Redeemer of the World; and, *then*, of the Blessing conveyed to us in the Sacrament from that Sacrifice.

First; the outward parts of this Sacrament fitly signify and represent to us the Passion of the LORD Himself. For this Bread and this Wine do not become Bread and Wine until the one has been cut down, beaten, ground, and baked with fire, and the other has been plucked off, bruised, and pressed out. The Life, we must observe, must first be *beaten and bruised out*. Even so, the SON of GOD does not become our SAVIOUR until He is cut down by death, bruised and wounded, and consumed as a Sacrifice, as it were, by the fire of Divine Justice. As the best corn is not bread, so long as it stands in the fields, so neither is the LORD JESUS made the Bread of Life to us, so long as He lives and teaches and works miracles, but only after He suffers, and is crucified, and dies. Nothing less than the Cross and the Passion of the SON of GOD makes Him to be our SAVIOUR, our very Bread of Life. As also the juice of the grape is not wine, so long as it is in the vine, so neither is the precious Blood of the Incarnate SON of GOD the very Water of Life to our souls, until it is all poured forth on the Cross, until it is all pressed out and shed in the tremendous Sacrifice. Whenever, therefore, we behold the outward Elements of Bread and Wine so solemnly used in this Sacrament, "*Jesus Christ is evidently set forth before our eyes crucified amongst us.*" (Gal. iii. 1.) Even the outward elements themselves significantly represent to our very senses the Cross and Passion of our LORD, the Sacrifice of the Son of GOD, the Bruising of the Great Redeemer.

Next, the outward parts are fitly chosen to signify and represent that inward and spiritual Blessing which is conveyed to us in the Sacrament. For Bread and Wine, we may well say, are the chief fruits of the earth, given us for the support and food of our bodily life: without Bread and Wine, without natural meat and drink, our bodily life would soon faint and decay. If we would live and be strong, then it is essential that we take continual supplies of earthly food. Even so, for our souls, some continual supply of spiritual food or sustenance, suitable to their nature, is required continually. And this food or sustenance is conveyed to us in this Sacrament, according to our LORD's own words: "*My Flesh is meat indeed, and My Blood is drink indeed.*" So that without this heavenly food, the very life of our souls grows weak and faint, and is ready to decay and perish; without frequent supplies of this spiritual and Divine meat and drink, "*we have no life in us.*"

Whenever, therefore, we come to this Holy Sacrament, the very outward parts of it most fitly and appropriately signify unto us that infinite Blessing which is herein conveyed to us in it, even the strengthening and refreshing of the very life of our souls by the Body and Blood of CHRIST, as our bodily life is strengthened and refreshed by natural bread and wine.

The outward parts of the Sacrament do thus therefore most appropriately signify and represent both the Sacrifice of the LORD's Death and also the very Food of our Eternal Life in Him.

THE USE OF THE OUTWARD ELEMENTS.

It was the custom of our LORD rather to build up His New Kingdom upon the foundation of the ancient Dispensations, than to begin everything afresh. He came, not to destroy the Law already given, but rather to fulfil it and make it perfect. He came to change the figure into the reality, the type into the antitype, the shadow into the substance. This truth we may perceive in our LORD's adoption of the fruits of the earth, Bread and Wine, to be the earthly materials of that one peculiar Service which He has left for our use during the whole of the Christian Dispensation. For by Divine Institution it had been customary all along, even from the beginning, to use these Fruits of the earth in the most solemn Acts of religious worship; and we cannot properly understand their singular use in the Holy Eucharist now, unless we understand their use in the former dispensations.

In the very first notice that we have of Sacrifices, we read that "*Cain brought of the fruit of the ground an offering unto the Lord;*" which offering S. Paul calls *a Sacrifice*. (Heb. xi. 4.) For anything brought and offered unto GOD, to be accepted by Him as an Act of Worship, is *a Sacrifice*. It need not of necessity be an animal to be slain, but it may be as well of the fruit of the earth; so that unbloody Sacrifices, as well as bloody Sacrifices, were offered in worship from the very first.

Then we read that the offering which Melchizedek brought forth as the Priest of GOD was distinctly an offering of Bread and Wine; and as we are taught both by Prophet and by Apostle that our LORD is a Priest "*according to the order of Melchizedek,*" we can easily perceive in this peculiar offering of Bread and Wine a Divinely-ordered prophecy and type of the use of these Fruits of the earth in the one distinctive Service instituted by our LORD.

But when we come to the Jewish Dispensation, in which every particular concerning Sacrifice was ordered by express Revelation, we find a still more peculiar and constant use of Bread and Wine.

There was then instituted "*a continual burnt-offering*," (Numb. xxviii. 1—8.) This consisted of two lambs, one sacrificed every morning, and the other every evening. But a meat-offering and a drink-offering were to accompany this Sacrifice; that is to say, an offering of flour with oil for the meat-offering, (rather meal-offering,) and of wine for the drink-offering. This peculiar offering of meal and wine was also commanded to accompany the other Sacrifices.

And here we should consider that the same custom prevailed even in heathen nations, having been received doubtless by tradition from some primeval source. This peculiar offering of flour and wine continually accompanied their Sacrifices. The meal and the wine were sprinkled and poured out on the animal to be sacrificed; and when that action had been done, the animal was reckoned as *already given and devoted to the Deity*.

So that the whole world was thus prepared by these Sacrificial Rites for the Christian Revelation. All were taught that worship by Sacrifice was the chief act of worship, and, moreover, that the Sacrifice was to be accompanied with an offering of meal and of wine.

The Life of some creature was to be offered, and the Offering was essentially connected with Bread and Wine.

Now our LORD, when about to institute the Holy Eucharist for the perpetual use of His Church, availed Himself of these Sacrificial Rites; or rather, we should say, He used them as already from the very first ordained and prepared by Himself. He carried on the use of these Fruits of the earth from the

Old into the New Dispensation, thus connecting the beginning with the ending, according to His own Divine Wisdom, and thus revealing to us what had been the real meaning and the prophetical character of those Sacrificial Rites all along.

Our LORD causes the Bread and the Wine to be the means of giving and offering the Sacrifice of His own Body and Blood, in a Heavenly Mystery, even before He actually suffered on the Cross. In that broken Bread and in that poured out Wine we see the realization of the ancient Offering which accompanied the slain Sacrifice. Our LORD mysteriously identifies the Unbloody Offering with the Bloody Sacrifice itself; for He says, "*This is My Body which is now being given to God in sacrifice for you.*" The very Sacrifice was begun. The Bread thus broken and given in the Holy Eucharist was made to carry and present the very sacrificed Body of the Lamb of GOD.[1]

And what the Holy Eucharist was made the means of doing *that night*, the same it is made the means of doing *still*, whenever it is celebrated.

The Bloody Sacrifice by actual Death was once, and once only, endured and offered; but that one Sacrifice is still carried and presented by the means here appointed by the LORD Himself. The Unbloody Offering of the Bread and the Wine carries and presents the one only real Sacrifice, the very Sacrifice of the LORD's most precious Body and Blood.

The heathen as well as the Jewish world had been Divinely prepared to receive this final Sacrificial Worship, by the very peculiar kind and mode of worship to which they had been accustomed all along, from the very first moment of the Fall of Man.

All had been taught to connect together the meal-offering and the drink-offering with the slain animal, the Bread and the Wine with the Sacrifice.

[1] This will be considered more at length in a following chapter.

The first use, then, of the outward elements in the Holy Eucharist is to be the means here below of carrying and presenting the One Sacrifice before GOD the FATHER. These Fruits of the earth, Bread and Wine, identified in a most profound heavenly mystery with the Body and the Blood of the One Sacrifice, are now appointed for the Church on earth, to be offered for "*the perpetual Memorial*" before GOD.

But another essential use of them remains to be considered. They not only carry and present the Sacrifice before GOD, but they also bring it to us, for our participation in it.

The exact use of the outward and visible parts of the Sacrament, in this second respect, is well expressed in our Church Catechism. The outward and visible Sign, it is there said, is ordained by CHRIST Himself, as a Means whereby we receive the inward and spiritual Grace, and as a Pledge to assure us thereof. The Bread and the Wine are ordained to be, in this respect, both *a Means* and *a Pledge*.

First, a Means. As S. Paul expresses it: "*The Bread, which we break, is the Communion,* [*or, the Participation*] *of the Body of Christ.*" The Bread, which is broken, and the Wine, which is blessed, in this Sacrament, are means, Divinely ordained, by which we are made partakers of the inward invisible Grace of the Sacrament; that is, of the Body and of the Blood of the LORD. There is no other way, no other means, expressly ordained and appointed by CHRIST, by which it is promised that we shall receive these inward and spiritual Gifts; but this is the means directly and expressly ordained for this special purpose.

And this, we may well here call to mind, has been a method often employed by GOD in dealing with man; to do some great work, or to give some great gift, by the means of some instrument which of itself was utterly powerless and weak. For instance, He divided the Red Sea, at or by the stroke of Moses' rod; He threw down the walls of Jericho, at or by the blowing of some trumpets; He cured Naaman of the leprosy, in or by the water of Jordan; He healed the sick woman, by the hem of His garment; He fed the multitude by means of a few small loaves; and so on. The weakness of the outward Sign, the utter insufficiency of the visible means, or instrument, or channel, only showed all the more plainly that in all such cases the excellency of the power was of GOD. But it pleased GOD to use such means; and it was doubtless intended thereby to try and prove and exercise our humility and our faith. The water of Jordan seemed to Naaman to be a means perfectly useless; but until he believed the Word of GOD, and humbled himself to obey it, he could find no cleansing.

So it is in this Sacrament of CHRIST: bread and wine have no power of their own, no virtue, to convey to us the Body and the Blood of CHRIST; but GOD ordains them, and commands us to receive them; and unless we humbly believe and obey, we have no promise given us, no other means appointed for us, whereby to receive those infinitely great and precious Gifts. The weakness of the outward Sign should not therefore offend us. This has been GOD's method all along—to produce great works, to give great gifts, by instruments and through means which, of themselves, are weak and utterly powerless, for the exercise of our humility and faith. GOD ever hides His great mysteries under lowly signs.

Next, the outward parts of the Sacrament are ordained as *a Pledge*, to assure us of the reception of the inward Grace. For the inward part of the Sacrament is spiritual, and heavenly, and invisible; it is not perceptible by any of our bodily senses; it is beyond all our human reason; it moves none of our present natural feelings. The Gifts given us in this Sacrament are supernatural, belonging to the Powers of Life and of Spirit; even the spiritual Substance of the Body and the Blood of the Incarnate LORD, the Second Adam. And our LORD expressly teaches us that these infinite Gifts are necessary to our salvation.

It is a matter, therefore, of the very utmost moment to us all, to know *where* we may have these Heavenly Gifts, to be made sure and certain that we do really and truly receive them. So that we might well feel convinced that our LORD would not leave us in any manner of doubtfulness on such an essential matter. He has Himself ordained certain Signs, as visible Pledges or Tokens, visible to our very bodily eye, perceptible by our very natural senses, in order to assure our inward faith, to make us sure and certain, that we do, then and there, take and receive His most precious Body and Blood. This is a provision of GOD'S mercy, on purpose to meet our wants, to suit our present state, to assure our hearts on a most vital point. As surely and as certainly as I take and receive the outward and visible Sign, even the Bread broken and consecrated in this Sacrament, so surely and certainly do I take and receive the Body of CHRIST in its invisible spiritual substance. As surely and as certainly as I take and drink this Cup, blessed in this Sacrament according to the LORD'S command, so surely and certainly do I take and receive the true and very Blood of CHRIST in its invisible essential substance.

Thus we have been left in no manner of uncertainty on this great matter. Our reception of the LORD'S most Blessed Body and Blood has been most perfectly provided for. The LORD Himself has ordained the Means and the Pledge. We all know perfectly *where to go* in order to receive the Heavenly Gifts. The Signs of their presence are indeed humble and lowly and weak to all outward appearance; but *this very Bread* is the Communion of the Body of CHRIST, *this very Cup* is the Communion of the Blood of CHRIST.

The outward visible parts of the Sacrament are thus ordained to be both a Means and a Pledge of our reception of the inward invisible parts of the Sacrament.

THE DIVINE PRESENCE HIDDEN UNDER LOWLY SIGNS.

" Verily, Thou art a God that hidest Thyself, O God of Israel, the Saviour." (Isa. xlv. 15.)

This ancient prophecy concerning the Redeemer of Israel is strikingly fulfilled in the Person and Kingdom of our LORD. GOD our SAVIOUR has been manifested in the flesh, and He is still *" God with us,"* and yet all along how has His Divine Presence been a hidden Presence. Here is one great part of the trying of our faith before GOD. His Presence is discerned, not by any outward glory, such as to overpower our bodily senses, but by faith only. Even in those cases in which the Presence of our LORD is most specially assured to us, and visible Signs of that special Presence are expressly appointed for the assurance of our faith, the Signs are only very humble and lowly Signs.

What was the Sign of the First Advent of the LORD from Heaven? When the Messiah actually came, by what Sign was He to be recognized? The Jews expected some grand Sign of His arrival, such as should astonish the whole world. But the Angel from Heaven said, *" This shall be the Sign."* What was the Sign of the actual Advent, of the visible Presence, of GOD our SAVIOUR? *A little Child lying in a manger.*

The LORD hid His great glory under this very humble and lowly Sign; so that the Jews, judging by nature only, all passed by the lowly throne, and saw therein nothing but a poor little human child. Never satisfied with the Signs of Divine Power which He gave them, they were ever still asking, *" What Sign showest Thou?"*

The real Presence of the LORD from Heaven was hidden from them under lowly Signs; Signs that none could receive unless they were walking humbly with their GOD, living by faith, and not by sight. For the whole Revelation of GOD to man is a trial of our humility and faith.

If we are proud, as Naaman was, we shall go away without any blessing, unwilling to believe in the appointed Sign.

It was not the great rushing rivers of Syria, but only the little silent stream of Israel, in which the Power of GOD was offered to the Syrian soldier for his cleansing; and until he humbly received that washing, he could find no relief. GOD hid His Power under that lowly Sign, to try the humility and the faith of the leper.

And when GOD would grant His special Presence to His Prophet Elijah, what was the Sign? Not the whirlwind, nor the earthquake, nor the fire; but the still small Voice.

And so the character of the present dispensation of Grace is still marked by this same thing.

The Presence of GOD our SAVIOUR is with us, but it is as yet a hidden Presence, hidden from our bodily senses, to be discerned by faith only, and marked by humble lowly Signs.

As at His Birth into our human family, GOD our SAVIOUR hid His Divine Glory under the weakness of our infancy, so He still hides His Presence amongst us under lowly Signs.

He has given us such promises of His special Presence as these—"*Where two or three are gathered together in My Name, there am I in the midst,*" thus promising to be specially present with all assemblies which are lawfully gathered together in His Name.

And to the Apostles and their successors in the Christian Priesthood, our LORD has given the special Promise, "*Lo, I am with you, alway, even to the end of the world.*"

And in His Holy Sacrament, our LORD says to us, "*This is My Body: This is My Blood.*" And we are very sure that the Presence of the LORD Himself cannot be separated from the Presence of His Body and Blood.

This last Promise is the one to which our present subject now confines our attention.

Here is the special Presence of the very Living Body and Blood of our LORD's Humanity, in an infinitely great Mystery; and therefore here is the special Presence of the very Person of our LORD.

On the Jewish Mercy Seat there was the special Presence of the Glory of the LORD; but on our Christian Altars there is the special Presence of the very Body and Blood of the Incarnate SON of GOD, infinitely more precious and glorious than that former cloud of glory.

But what is the appointed sign of this Divine Presence? The sign that is visible to the bodily senses is only humble and lowly indeed; for it is nothing more than a little Bread and Wine. The LORD's Presence is verily and indeed here, but it is vailed under very lowly outward signs. A little child lying in the manger was the lowly sign of the LORD's first Presence amongst us; and now the sign of His Presence amongst us in the Holy Eucharist is nothing more or greater than Bread and Wine. The Divine Presence is here, but hidden under these signs.

In that stable at Bethlehem, our natural senses told us only, "*Here is a little human child;*" but our faith told us, "*Here is the Presence of the Lord from Heaven.*"

In the Holy Eucharist, our natural senses say only, "*Here is Bread and Wine;*" but our faith discerns the invisible reality, and says, "*Here is the Body and the Blood of the Incarnate Son of God.*"

Whenever we come to the Holy Eucharist, therefore, there is a trying of our faith, whether we *discern the Lord's Body*, or no. The outward sign is mean, and poor, and lowly to the eyes of sense; to the eyes of faith, it is the appointed sign of the real Divine Presence.

WORSHIP BY SACRIFICE.

"Gather My saints together unto Me: those that have made a Covenant with Me with Sacrifice." (Ps. l. 5.)

It is certainly one of the most remarkable and at the same time one of the most important facts relating to this world, that every religion since the Creation has had for its chief Act of Worship, *Worship by Sacrifice*. The highest and the most essential Act of Worship has ever and everywhere been believed to consist in some kind of Sacrifice; in some instances those Sacrifices having been even *human* Sacrifices.

Many attempts have been made by learned men to account for the origin and the reason of this most striking fact. But for the Believer in the Christian Revelation, there is no difficulty in understanding it. It is indeed itself one of the strongest arguments for the truth of the Christian Religion. For GOD alone could foreknow that Infinite Sacrifice by which the world should be redeemed, and so none but He could institute so singular a mode of Worship for fallen man as Worship by Sacrifice.

We Christians can now perceive in the very first Promise of the Redeemer of the World, (Gen. iii. 15,) the real foundation and the deep significance of the whole Institution of *Worship by Sacrifice;* because the Redemption of a fallen World was to be accomplished by the "*bruising*" of the Redeemer; so that this One great Sacrifice, thus foretold from the beginning, became at once the Hope of all the World, the special Object of Faith for every Believer in GOD, and the very Centre of all acceptable Worship.

And then also, when we look onwards, (Rev. v. 12,) even to the full accomplishment of all the glories of the Redeemer's Kingdom, when Satan shall be bruised under our feet for ever; all those eternal glories are revealed as having their centre in the Throne of "*the Lamb that was slain.*"

If then the very earliest Worship of fallen man pointed to that One Divine Sacrifice; and if the eternal Worship of the glorified Church will ever have respect to that One Divine Sacrifice, surely it needs not a word to convince us that the present Worship of the Church Militant must also have this One Divine Sacrifice as its chief and central object.

In the complicated and manifold Laws concerning Sacrifice, which were given to the Jewish Church, we learn all the various ends and purposes for which the One True Sacrifice serves; for all the various kinds of Sacrifices then instituted are fulfilled in all perfection in that One which they all prefigured.

But in the single and simple Form in which Worship by Sacrifice existed in the first Patriarchal Age, we perceive the one fundamental meaning of all Sacrifice; for it pleased GOD at the beginning to reveal distinctly only the groundwork of that system of Sacrifices which was afterwards more fully given by Moses; in order that the world might be educated, by degrees, from the first, so as to be able with less difficulty to receive the Mysteries of the Kingdom of CHRIST.

Worship by Sacrifice, then, we must remember, was not a Jewish Ordinance alone; it was not a distinctive part of the Mosaic Law; it existed before from the very beginning; even from the creation of the world Worship by Sacrifice had formed the one distinctive feature of the Religion which GOD had appointed for fallen man; it was the Worship of the Old World before the deluge; it was the Worship of Noah and his sons; it was the Worship of all Believers in GOD, before the time of Moses. And it spread of course from the first fountain-head through all the generations and nations of the world; and it still exists, in some shape or other, even amongst nations where the true meaning of it has been quite lost or perverted. Even in heathen nations, widely separated from one another, so many of the main rites of Sacrifice, even in some minute particulars, still exist, that nothing can give any satisfactory account of the fact, except that the whole world learnt from primeval Institution the notion and the mode of Sacrificial Worship. Whether to the True GOD or to false gods, Worship by Sacrifice was universally believed to be the chief mode of Worship. Worship by Sacrifice was the very sum and substance, the very soul and centre of the Religion of the whole world.

From the very first, Holy Scripture records the fact, that Worship by means of Sacrifice was emphatically the Worship of GOD, the peculiar worship which GOD appointed and accepted.

We, Christians, enlightened with the Light of the Gospel, can now perceive the infinitely great reason and meaning of this universal existence of Sacrificial Worship.

Let us place ourselves by the side of one of the Sacrifices in the Patriarchal Age, when Sacrifice was offered in its very simplest and most elementary form. Here is an animal brought to the Altar of GOD; it is slain; its blood, which is its life, is poured out before GOD; its body is laid upon the Altar and wholly consumed by fire. What words were used in offering the Sacrifice, if any, we do not know: nor is it necessary; *the action itself speaks;* the action is the essential part of the Worship; the action itself it is which really pleads before GOD. What then is its value? what is its real significance? what is the reason that every Believer in GOD, in all his chief acts of worship, approaches GOD in this most peculiar Form of Worship?

We, enlightened with Christian Faith, understand the great Mystery, hidden under this outward Form, more clearly than the ancient Patriarchs did. "We do this, (we might have said,) we offer this Sacrifice, before GOD, in figure and type of that One tremendous and all-atoning Sacrifice which He has promised, which is coming, when the Great Redeemer shall be bruised for our sins, in which Sacrifice we trust, by means of which alone we thus venture into the Presence of GOD; which One Sacrifice we do here represent and set forth before the Divine Majesty, in His own appointed way, as our one only Plea, our one chief Act of Worship. In this bleeding Sacrifice we behold by faith the Sacrifice of the very Lamb of GOD; by this means we set before the eyes of GOD the very Sacrifice of His SON, worshipping Him thereby, offering to Him that Sacrifice to be the Propitiation for our sins, putting Him in remembrance of His own Promise, praying by this appointed means for an interest in that One True Divine Sacrifice which is coming."

The chief particulars introduced by the Law of Moses were these; the Act of offering a Sacrifice was restricted to the office of the Priesthood, which was then distinctly instituted in its threefold Order. So that the truth might be instilled by figure and type, that for the True Sacrifice which was coming, a Great High Priest was required; and also that the threefold Order of the Christian Priesthood might be foreshadowed.

Four distinctions were made in the Sacrifices themselves, according to the four different objects for which Sacrifice may be offered; namely, *Burnt-offerings*, to give supreme honour and worship to GOD; *Thank-offerings*, to give GOD thanks and praise for all His gifts to us; *Sin-offerings*, to pray for pardon of sin and guilt; and *Peace-offerings*, to ask of GOD those Blessings of which we stand in need.

Then also were distinctly introduced, by Divine Institution, *Unbloody Sacrifices*, such as, Sacrifices of flour, oil, frankincense, &c., and in cases of poverty even a Sin-offering might be offered in an unbloody Sacrifice of flour. But in all these unbloody Sacrifices we must notice that it was commanded that *the Life* should be offered, the corn must be beaten out to flour, the grape must be pressed out to wine, &c., the *living power* must be destroyed in the Sacrifice; there must still be shown forth the great Mystery of the "*bruising*" in the Sacrifice. It was also then expressly instituted that there should be always an Offering of Flour and of Wine to accompany even the Bloody Sacrifices; prefiguring the Bread and the Wine which the Divine Priest Himself, as our true Melchizedec, should afterwards appoint to be the earthly materials for His one only distinctive Service, to carry His own Divine Sacrifice, to be the means by which the One Tremendous Sacrifice is now everywhere offered in memorial before GOD.

Moreover there then came in the peculiar appointment that the Priest and the Offerer of the Sacrifice were to be *partakers of the Sacrifice*; so that there might be a kind of Holy Banquet before GOD, a Feast upon the Sacrifice, a Holy Communion.

And, lastly, there was instituted the great Day of Atonement once a year, when the High Priest alone entered in, before the special Presence of GOD, carrying in with him the Blood of the Sacrifice, which he was to sprinkle, for Propitiation and Atonement for sin, on and before the innermost Altar of GOD, that so all the Sacrifices of the whole year might be accepted and completed, an Atonement for all their sins once a year being thus made.

And all these things were expressly ordained, we must ever bear in mind, as examples and shadows upon earth of Heavenly things, (Heb. viii. 5.) In every rite and ceremony there was some likeness to the Heavenly Reality to which it corresponded. The whole Divine Service upon earth was a true figure and outline, for the time then present, of those Holy Mysteries which are now revealed and given to us in the Church of CHRIST; every part of it is now fulfilled by the everliving Priesthood and Sacrifice of the LORD CHRIST, in the worship of the Heavenly Court within the veil and in the worship on earth beneath: for all the whole Church is one in Him.

All these Institutions are written in the first seven chapters of Leviticus, and in the 29th of Exodus.

Sacrifice, therefore, in one way or another, was the very soul and centre of the Worship which GOD thus commanded to be given Him. Every morning and every evening, all the year round, a Lamb was offered in Sacrifice, with its offering of Flour and of Wine, and with Incense. On the Sabbath, this Sacrifice was doubled. Every New Moon, still more Sacrifices were appointed. All the great yearly Festivals were marked with still more Sacrifices. And not only so, for Public Worship, but also for individuals; if any one committed sin, he had to make confession of it and to offer Sacrifice; or if any one desired some Blessing, he brought a Sacrifice; or if he desired to return Thanks, he brought a Sacrifice. So that Sacrifice was the one great and distinguishing Act of their Religion, the distinctive and the continuous religious Action of their lives.

From Adam then up to the Deluge, and then onward to Moses, extending itself through all the tribes of mankind, and then more fully than ever in the Jewish dispensation, *Worship by Sacrifice* was the distinctive Religion appointed for fallen man.

In the most expanded state of Sacrificial Worship under the Mosaic Revelation, there was one continual Offering of Sacrifices; it was so every day of the year, and on every chief occasion, public or private. The Fire upon the Altar of GOD was never to go out; the Smoke of the Sacrifices never ceased; the Sweet Savour was always ascending up to Heaven; the Blood of the Victims was ever being sprinkled before the LORD.

And all this was to train and educate the whole world in Sacrificial Worship; in order to prepare us all for the present Christian Dispensation; all this was fore-ordained, to help us to receive the Mysteries of the Kingdom of GOD Incarnate. All along, we see, it has been One continual Worship by means of Sacrifice, all showing forth the Bruising of the Great Redeemer, all prefiguring the One only real and true Sacrifice; the presentation of Which, in one way or another, by one means or another, was of necessity, the soul and centre of Worship for fallen man. Fallen man can approach GOD acceptably in no age or nation, except only by the all-atoning Sacrifice of CHRIST.

If we would now offer Worship, for the Glory and Honour of GOD, we offer the Sacrifice of His Eternal SON, the only true and perfect Sacrifice, the one that renders infinite Glory to GOD Himself; in union with which alone it is that we can offer acceptably our own poor imperfect unworthy worship.

If we would render Thanks for all the Gifts of GOD to us, we offer the Sacrifice of His Eternal SON, as That unspeakable Gift which comprehends all others, in union with which our Thanksgiving can alone be acceptable.

If we would pray for Pardon of sin, we offer the all-atoning Sacrifice of the Lamb of GOD, the one True Sin-offering, which alone is the Propitiation for the sins of the world, reconciling GOD to us and us to GOD.

If we would ask for any Blessing, we offer the Sacrifice of GOD's Eternal SON, making That our only plea, the only ground of our prayers.

Here, then, of course, the great Question may well arise in our minds, Are we Christians now *left to ourselves* as to the manner or means of offering our chief Acts of Worship? Or, is there now *any Divinely instituted Form of Worship*, for our central Worship, corresponding in any manner to that which GOD appointed for man before the coming of CHRIST?

The answer to this great Question is found in the positive Institution of the Holy Eucharist by our LORD Himself, to be the one distinctive and central Act of Worship for His whole Church, even till He come again: one most essential reason for which Divine Institution, is this very thing, that we may have a Means, not invented by ourselves, but distinctly ordained by GOD Himself when manifest in the flesh by which we may show forth the Sacrifice of the death of CHRIST, as our central Act of Worship.

And here also we cannot but consider and believe that any Institution of this kind, given under the present Christian dispensation, must needs be one of higher glory and greater dignity and richer grace than any of those in former ages. For *they* were only for figures and types; we have the very substance and reality.

A worshipper standing by the Altar of GOD in the introductory dispensation, might have said, "Here I behold the body of a lamb, offered on the Altar by slaughter and fire; here is the life-blood of a sacrifice poured out before GOD; but all this is only a figure of what is coming, all this is but a type of what GOD has promised: all this is only a shadow of the great reality on which my faith is fixed: I offer this only as a Sign of something absent; I do this as a figure of something future."

But a worshipper standing now by the Altar of GOD in the Church of CHRIST, may say, "Here I see no Bloody Victim: here I offer the Body of no animal: here I present no mere figure, no mere shadow, no mere type of something future, no empty Sign of something absent; but here I offer That of which it is said by the True Priest Himself, '*This is My Body;*' here I present That of which the LORD says, '*This is My Blood.*' Here is present, verily and indeed, not the shadow, but the Substance; not the sign only, but the Thing signified also: not the type, but the very Antitype: not a bare sign of something absent, but the true Sign of something present: here is present on the Holy Altar the Body and the Blood of the True Lamb of GOD, the very Sacrifice of CHRIST Himself: here in a most profound reality is the Divine Victim as It had been slain: here is the one ever Sacrifice, in a most Heavenly Mystery of Truth."

Thus we Christians still *worship by Sacrifice*. This is our *one central worship*. There never was any other, and never can be any other. Only, now we have the very Sacrifice itself made present on our Altars by Divine Power in a most holy and heavenly Mystery. Now the very Lamb of GOD, who stands as It had been slain before the Presence of the FATHER in the Sanctuary above before the Heavenly Altar itself, is nevertheless present on all the Altars of the Church on earth, in every Holy Eucharist.

Now the true Sacrifice is ever being presented; above and below : now the true Mercy-Seat within the vail is ever being sprinkled with the Blood of the Lamb in Heavenly truth and reality: now the Tremendous Sacrifice is ever smoking through Heaven and Earth: now the One Offering and Sacrifice is ever going up in its Sweet Savour before the Presence of the FATHER.

THE PRIESTHOOD AFTER THE ORDER OF MELCHIZEDEC.

One of the clearest and most remarkable revelations ever made under the Old Testament Dispensation, concerning the Person and the Offices of our LORD, is that which is given in the 110th Psalm. The FATHER is there represented by the Prophet as speaking to the SON, constituting Him both King and Priest.

The only part of this Prophecy which belongs to our present subject, is that in which the nature of the Priesthood of our LORD is revealed; "*The Lord sware, and will not repent, Thou art a Priest for ever after the order of Melchizedec.*" The everlasting Priesthood of the Messiah, conferred upon Him with the immutable oath of the FATHER, is, according to this ancient Prophecy, a Priesthood, not according to the Order of Aaron, but according to the Order of Melchizedec.

To this most remarkable and clear Prophecy S. Paul

repeatedly refers, when he is writing concerning the Priesthood of our LORD, in the fifth and seventh chapters of his Epistle to the Hebrews, in which he proves the superiority of the Priesthood of our LORD over the Jewish Priesthood, by means of the history of Melchizedec.

Since then it is so expressly and strikingly revealed to us that the Priesthood of Melchizedec was the Type which foreshadowed our LORD's Priesthood, in some peculiar and essential respects, even rather than the Priesthood of Aaron, it is most necessary that we should consider this with all possible care.

The account which is given us of Melchizedec in Holy Scripture (Gen. xiv.) was doubtless so ordered as to signify to us, through the explanation given by S. Paul, the special points in which the Priesthood of our LORD should excel the Priesthood of Aaron. And this is done by the designed *silence* of Holy Scripture, as well as by what is *actually related*, concerning Melchizedec. We must mark in the account of this eminent Type of the Messiah, not only what is *said*, but as well what is designedly *not said;* following the guidance of S. Paul in his seventh chapter. For the very *silence* of Holy Scripture is sometimes most expressive to every thoughtful mind.

Melchizedec then is brought before us as a Priest of GOD, having no Predecessor and no Successor, the only one of his peculiar Order; there is, in the account given of him, no human pedigree, no father, no mother; no beginning of his days mentioned, nor any end of his life. Thus, so far as the account of Holy Scripture designedly informs us, he is "*made like,*" by Divine foreknowledge, "*unto the Son of God,*" and "*abideth a Priest continually.*" One glance only, as it were, is given us of Melchizedec; and in it we see him, alone in his Order, performing one priestly action only; and then, the single glance is withdrawn. The one ever abiding, continual, unchangeable Priesthood of our LORD, was thus foreshadowed.

After the Order of Aaron, there were many successive Priests; after the Order of Melchizedec, there was only one Priest, without any before or after him; and he only performed one priestly action.

What then is this one priestly action performed by Melchizedec? This we must consider with the utmost concern; because here doubtless was foreshadowed another special difference between our LORD's Priesthood and that of Aaron.

If Melchizedec did offer slain animals in sacrifice, it is not related: it is designedly passed over in sacred and expressive silence; for in that point would not have consisted the distinguishing difference, nor the peculiar excellence, of the Priestly Action of the Messiah.

But what *is* the account of the one Priestly action of Melchizedec? He brought forth not any living animal to be slain and offered in sacrifice; but he brought forth Fruits of the earth, Bread and Wine; and so, as Priest of the Most High GOD, he blessed Abraham, the Father of the Faithful.

Now by blessing the Patriarch Abraham, it was distinctly shown forth that the Priesthood existing among the Patriarchs, and the Levitical Priesthood also, (Heb. vii. 10,) ought to be considered as inferior to that other Priesthood which was foreshadowed by that of Melchizedec.

But the chief point which belongs to our subject is this: that the Scriptural account only relates the Offering of the Bread and the Wine. All else is kept out of view and passed over in designed silence. This, therefore, which *is* related, must be a main point; here is that distinguishing feature of the Order of Melchizedec which expressly foreshadowed the peculiar action of the Messiah's Priesthood. If our LORD had been called to be a Priest after the Order of Aaron, He would still, like Aaron, offer continually upon earth slain animals, as Memorials of His Sacrifice of Himself: but, being called to be a Priest after the

Order of Melchizedec, He brings forth only Fruits of the earth, the Bread and the Wine.

Melchizedec, then, foreshadowed, in the one only Action related of him, the very peculiar and distinguishing Action of our Great High Priest Himself. For at the Institution of the One only great and distinguishing Service of the Christian Dispensation, the LORD the Priest brings forth only Bread and Wine; He consecrates these Fruits of the earth to be the means of the one abiding Offering of the New Law, until He should come again.

At the Holy Institution of this New Rite, which was to supersede all preceding ones, the LORD Himself begins to execute His Office as our true and very Melchizedec. He begins upon earth, in a Holy Mystery, that very Sacrifice of Himself which was finished on the Cross in Blood and Death, and then was carried in, on the Ascension, within the veil and offered before the true Mercy Seat. For He brings forth Bread and Wine; He blesses and consecrates these Fruits of the earth, for spiritual, heavenly uses; of the one, He says, "*This is My Body;*" and of the other, "*This is My Blood.*"

By this means, our Great High Priest, beginning His unchangeable Priesthood after the Order of Melchizedec, offers no figure, no type, but verily and indeed, Himself, to the FATHER, in sacrifice for our sins; He "*gives*" to Him His Body and His Blood "*for us*" under these visible Signs, these long-prefigured Symbols.

The body and the blood of slain animals, which were offered under the old Covenant, were now for ever to disappear: the Order of the Priesthood was to be changed; and, instead, the Blood of the New Covenant was to be present; the Body and the Blood of the very Lamb of GOD were to be present, in a Heavenly Mystery, under these visible Signs and Forms of Bread and Wine.

The bloody Offerings of slain animals which were

offered by the Priesthood of the Patriarchal and Judaical Orders, were no longer to be types and shadows and figures of the One Sacrifice; but the One Sacrifice Itself was to be ever present and ever offered beneath these sacred signs and vails, according to the New Order of Melchizedec.

For that which our LORD Himself *began* to do, at that first Institution of the Holy Eucharist, He *continues* still to do upon earth by the hands of His appointed Priests. For what *they* do by His Command and Authority, He Himself does, in Divine power and Heavenly reality. At ten thousand Altars He continually discharges His unchangeable Priesthood, as our true Melchizedec, bringing forth the Bread and the Wine, and causing them to be, in Holy and tremendous Mystery, His Body and His Blood, to show forth the Sacrifice of His death before the FATHER, and then to be given to us for our Spiritual Food and Sustenance, to refresh the fainting life of our souls in the midst of our terrible warfare in this present evil world.

Thus then we see in that one only Action of Melchizedec a perfect type and image of the Holy Eucharist, the Pure Oblation of the Gospel Dispensation, the one only Service ordered for us all by the LORD CHRIST Himself, to be our distinctive Act of Worship till He come again.

Our LORD, as a Priest after the Order of Melchizedec, we must remember, executes His Office *here upon earth;* for *in heaven*, it is plain, He does not bring forth Bread and Wine. It is in His Church on earth that our Great High Priest thus executes His Melchizedeckian Priesthood.

And thus, both above and below, He Alone is really the One true Priest, ever ministering for us before the FATHER, both there and here; there, in His own Visible Person, here below, by the hands of His visible Priests and by visible Signs; ever showing forth the One Sacrifice of His own Body and of His own Blood.

All the bloody Sacrifices of former ages have ceased: no priest according to the Order of Aaron remains; but the Incarnate SON of GOD is Himself made a Priest for ever after the Order of Melchizedec; bringing forth, by the hands of His Ministers upon earth, to the end of time, Bread and Wine; whereby to show forth the Sacrifice of Himself before the FATHER.

This is therefore our one distinctive Act of Christian Worship.

In this Act, we call into action, more than in any other, our LORD's everlasting continual Priesthood; in this Act we are raised up into a present participation of His continual ministrations above. Here, by His own Command, and in His own way, we all upon earth do the same thing as He Himself does in Heaven above; we show forth, we present, we lift up, we plead, the One Eternal Sacrifice. Thus we use and receive the One only Atonement for sins.

THE PASSOVER.

"And when the hour was come, He sat down, and the twelve Apostles with Him. And He said unto them, With desire I have desired to eat this Passover with you before I suffer. For I say unto you, I will not any more eat thereof, until it be fulfilled in the kingdom of God." (S. Luke xxii. 14—16.)

Our LORD having perfect knowledge of all things, ever ordering all things from the beginning to the end in Divine Wisdom, chose the conclusion of this last Passover Supper to be the occasion on which to institute the Holy Sacrament of our Redemption.

From this very circumstance therefore we receive instruction. By the very selection of this occasion on which to institute this Sacrament our LORD teaches us.

As soon as that last Passover Supper was ended, (S. Luke xxii. 20,) our LORD put into its place to the end of time the Holy Eucharist. So that when the ancient Passover had been fulfilled by the Sacrifice of Himself the true Paschal Lamb, and when the New Kingdom of GOD had come, there remained no longer the ancient type, but this Holy Sacrament in its stead, for all succeeding generations, even till the LORD should come in glory.

We might well here call to mind, how often our LORD was wont to take something that already existed and to build upon it, rather than introduce something altogether unknown. For instance, in the case of the other Holy Sacrament, our LORD did not introduce a Rite altogether new, but He rather took what He found already existing, the Water-baptisms then in use, and so instituted thereupon His own Sacrament of Baptism; thus destroying nothing, but rather fulfilling what existed with Heavenly Grace, consecrating it and raising it to a higher use in His New Kingdom.

It is therefore very needful for the right understanding of the Holy Eucharist, that we should look back and examine the ancient foundation on which it is built. An attentive consideration of the type greatly assists us to enter into the full significance of the Antitype.

That the Old Testament was a Divinely intended Figure of the New, no one doubts. Just as in the history of the Creation of Adam and Eve we may see distinctly foreshadowed "*the great Mystery of Christ and His Church,*" (Eph. v. 32,) even so all the most remarkable events and ordinances which are recorded by the HOLY GHOST in the Old Testament have a Divinely intended relation, in the way of prophecy and type, to the greater events and ordinances belonging to CHRIST and His Church under the New Testament.

The leading type of the Old Testament consists in the history of the children of Israel. GOD so ordered all that history that it should be a most instructive shadow and type of all that chiefly concerns us in the

Church of CHRIST, as indeed S. Paul expressly declares in 1 Cor. x. 1—12.

Thus therefore the miraculous Redemption of the Israelites out of their fallen state in Egypt was an eminent figure and type of the Redemption of the world from the curse of a fallen state by CHRIST Himself; and the means which were then ordered to be used for that typical redemption were figures Divinely foreordained of what was to take place, in the fulness of time, in the true Redemption itself.

The Sacrifice and Feast of the Passover was instituted the same night in which that typical redemption began to take place; or rather that redemption took place in consequence of that Sacrifice; and the Service then instituted remained as a standing Memorial of that deliverance throughout the whole of the Jewish Dispensation, even up to the very night in which our true Redemption itself began to be accomplished, by the actual fulfilment of that which was typified in the ancient Passover.

Now the ancient Passover may be briefly described thus: The Israelites, the night in which they began their march out of Egypt, were commanded to kill and sacrifice an unblemished Lamb, in all their families, to sprinkle their door-posts with the blood of the sacrifice, as a sign for the destroying Angel to pass over their houses; and then they were to eat in their houses the flesh of the sacrificed Lamb roasted with fire, with unleavened bread and bitter herbs, having their loins girt up, their shoes on their feet and their staves in their hands. And this Divinely ordained Service was to be most exactly observed by every Israelite, in all their generations, on pain of excommunication from the congregation of Israel.

This Holy Ordinance therefore remained as one of the most distinguishing Rites of the whole Jewish Dispensation. For any one to profess the Jewish Religion and not keep the Passover, was unheard of.

The Divine Command was absolute: "Thou shalt

sacrifice the Passover unto the LORD thy GOD, that thou mayest remember the day when thou camest forth out of the land of Egypt all the days of thy life. It is the Sacrifice of the LORD'S Passover."

And this Command was obligatory on pain of excommunication from the congregation of the LORD. (Numb. ix. 13.)

But this illustrious and ancient Ordinance was only a forerunner and figure of something better than itself. It was only a shadow of a substance which should be revealed in the fulness of time. It was expressly foreordained of GOD in order to prepare the world for the Mysteries of CHRIST and His Church; for in the Type the nature of the Antitype was distinctly marked out and foreshown in its main particulars; and even now, by looking back and considering the Type, our own minds are greatly enlightened and confirmed in Christian faith and knowledge.

Let us mark the *three* main points in this ancient Institution. (See Exod. xii. and Deut. xvi.)

I. A Lamb without blemish or spot was to be offered for Sacrifice at GOD'S holy Altar by all the Israelites.

II. The Blood of the Lamb, which is its Life, being then shed and offered in sacrifice to GOD, its Body was then to be eaten by all the Israelites.

III. The whole Service was to be continued as a perpetual Memorial for all their generations, of their Redemption out of Egypt, and as a very distinctive Act of Worship before GOD, to give Him thanks for that miraculous deliverance.

Now this shadow has passed away, and the substance itself has come; the type has been fulfilled, the Antitype is ours in the New Kingdom of GOD.

I. The true and very Lamb of GOD, the Incarnate Word, has been slain and offered in sacrifice unto GOD, for the redemption of the world. " *Christ, our Passover, is sacrificed for us.*"

II. He is not only "*given*" in Sacrifice to GOD *for*

us, but He is also given *to us*, to be the true spiritual food and sustenance of our eternal life.

III. A Holy Ordinance is Divinely instituted as a standing Memorial of our Redemption by the Blood of the very Lamb of GOD. For the same night in which our LORD began to die for us, having closed the Old Testament Dispensation by celebrating the solemnities of the Jewish Passover for the last time, (for that night was the beginning of the day on which the Paschal Lamb was commanded to be killed,) He instituted the New Rite of the Christian Dispensation. He turned the Jewish ceremonies into a Christian Sacrament; He took the Fruits of the earth which were then used at the Passover Supper, Bread and Wine, and blessed them to a higher use in His New Kingdom, and made them signs and pledges of the Presence of the very Body and Blood of the True Paschal Lamb; "*giving*," by these holy Mysteries, even then, Himself "*for us*" in sacrifice to GOD; and then also giving Himself *to us* in the Holy Communion of His Body and Blood; thus, under the New Rite of His own Church, fulfilling the ancient Type of the Passover in heavenly reality; and commanding this Mystical Sacrifice and Holy Communion to be kept up for ever, as our Great Thanksgiving for the Redemption of the World by His Blood, and as the means of our individual Participation in all the Benefits of His Sacrifice; so that he who partakes not of this Holy Communion should be "*cut off*" from the congregation of the LORD, having no longer Eternal Life abiding in him.

In this Holy Sacrament of the Eucharist, therefore, which our LORD thus so strikingly put into the place of the ancient Passover on that most memorable night, when our true Redemption began by the shedding of His own Blood, we have the very truth and reality which were so clearly marked out and foreshown by Divine foreknowledge in the institution of the Jewish Passover; for here, CHRIST our true Paschal Lamb is first of all "*given*" or offered unto GOD "*for us*," as our one only and true Sacrifice; and then He is also given *unto us* to be partaken of in the Holy Communion of His most precious Body and Blood; in order that the Benefits of the Sacrifice of the Lamb of GOD may be all communicated to our souls; the very Grace purchased for us by our true Redeemer being thus given and assured to every one who partakes "*worthily*," that is to say, with the unleavened bread of sincerity and truth, with the bitter but wholesome herbs of repentance and mortification of sin, with the affections of his mind girt up and restrained from earthly things, his feet shod in readiness for pursuing his great journey, and the staff of his hasty pilgrimage in his hand.

We plainly learn, therefore, from the characteristic features of this ancient type, that in the Holy Eucharist, which our LORD has now put in the place of the Passover, there must be *two* chief truths ever borne in mind by us; the Sacrifice of the death of the true Paschal Lamb is first of all shown forth and pleaded before GOD in holy Mysteries; and then we are made partakers of the Sacrifice, by spiritually eating His Flesh and drinking His Blood. For we cannot be mistaken in our belief that this type is fulfilled in the Kingdom of GOD; all shadows have passed away; the Jewish Passover is turned into the Christian Eucharist. The Paschal Lamb, first given in sacrifice to GOD, and then eaten by the Israelites, is now replaced, in heavenly truth and holy mystery, in this true Sacrament of our Redemption, not by any new figure or shadow, but by the Reality itself; for at every Celebration of this distinctive Act of the Christian Religion, the LORD Himself makes good His own words: "*Take; eat: this is My Body, which is given for you.*" This is the New Passover which CHRIST Himself has instituted in the New Kingdom of GOD, the very Antitype of the ancient typical Passover in the kingdom of Israel.

OUR LORD'S ACTIONS AND WORDS AT THE INSTITUTION.

If we would rightly understand the nature of this Divine Institution, it must be plain that in the very first place it is necessary that we should consider with all possible care and reverential attention, *that which our Lord Himself did*, and *that which our Lord Himself said*, at the time of the Institution itself. For the Actions and the Words which our LORD then used must contain the very Truth of GOD concerning this holy Mystery. Let us humbly consider them separately, that we may the more easily give them all their due significance. For every Word and every Action, at the Institution, we cannot but hold was full of significance. They were all intended to give meaning and force to the Institution, even to the end of time. These Actions and these Words of our LORD must contain the Divine Foundation of all that we are obliged to believe concerning the Holy Eucharist.

I. "*Jesus took Bread, and blessed it.*" So S. Paul writes of the Cup: "*The Cup of Blessing, which we bless.*"

Here we must consider what *Blessing the Bread* means; for this is the first Action of our LORD in instituting the true Passover. We must not confound this *Blessing of the Bread and of the Cup* with what we commonly mean by "*Saying Grace*" before a common meal. For this was not by any means a common meal; and besides we observe that our LORD not only Blessed the Bread, but that He also "*Gave Thanks*" over this Bread and this Cup, and this took place *before* the Disciples partook of them.

The greatness of the occasion rather leads us at once to connect this Blessing of the creature by the Creator with other cases where He was wont to Bless them. Such as that original Blessing of all creatures: "*God Blessed them, and God said unto them, Be fruitful and multiply;*" the force of which Divine Benediction has been perpetual ever since in all creatures.

Especially ought we to connect this peculiar Act of our LORD with some similar ones that are recorded in the Gospels. For we find that on two occasions it is expressly written that our LORD blessed creatures, and gave thanks over them. In S. Luke ix. 16, we read that "*He took the five loaves and the two fishes, and looking up to Heaven, He blessed them, and brake, and gave to the Disciples to set before the multitude;*" and the miraculous effect produced by this Divine Blessing was that the Loaves and the Fishes were so multiplied as to satisfy all the people. The other occasion was a similar one; and on Blessing the seven loaves and the few small fishes, they were so multiplied as to become food enough for four thousand people. In this case S. Mark writes that our LORD also "*Gave Thanks*" before the miraculous increase, and S. John tells us that the same *Giving of Thanks* took place in the other similar Miracle.

That there was something very peculiar in this Action of our LORD is also evident from the circumstance that the Disciples at Emmaus did not recognise our LORD until *He took bread and blessed it*. That Action it was which opened their eyes, and caused them to perceive Who it was. "*He was known of them in Breaking of Bread.*"

That some very peculiar and miraculous Gift, that is to say, some supernatural and Divine effect should follow this *Blessing of the Bread and of the Cup*, we can therefore hardly fail to understand and believe. What this miraculous effect and Divine Gift was, the words then spoken reveal to us. For after the LORD had given thanks over the Bread and Wine and had blessed them, then He said of them, "*This is My Body,*" and "*This is My Blood.*"

Now this Blessing, and this Effect of it, remain *ever the same,* even to the end of the present dispensation; just as the force of that Original Blessing of all Creatures remains ever the same for all their generations.

As the words once spoken, "*Increase and multiply,*" have their effect to-day just as powerfully and truly as when first spoken, so it is also with the Words, "*This is My Body;*" they were spoken by GOD manifest in the flesh but once, but they are made good by Him in all ages of His Church. What the Holy Sacrament was at first, such it continues to be, always, even to the end of the world. Every Eucharist is the same as the first one.

So that it becomes a matter of the very utmost consequence to us to believe rightly these Divine Words.

II. "*This is My Body.*"

These Divine Words should be received and understood by us in the most exact and careful way possible. For being spoken by our LORD on so great an occasion, they could not have been Words hastily chosen. Our LORD perfectly knew what human Words were most suitable and exact for His purpose; He also foreknew that they would be used at every Celebration of this Holy Mystery throughout His whole Church to the end of the present dispensation. We cannot therefore believe that any one Word here used was used without choice; we cannot but believe that they are all absolutely perfect Words, that is to say, so far as any human words can be perfect, when they are used to express a heavenly Mystery. For a Mystery they doubtless contain, which reaches above and beyond the limits of our present knowledge. But this Mystery they express as perfectly as any human words can do.

We may not surely alter the Words, or change them for others in any the slightest way whatever.

We may not add unto them, nor diminish from them, but rather take them just as the LORD Himself has spoken them once for all.

For instance, we must not, on peril of using the Word of GOD deceitfully, put any such interpretation on these Divine Words as would be equivalent to our putting into the midst of them the word "not," and so making them really mean, "*This is not My Body.*"

Now this danger we may easily fall into, if we permit ourselves to interpret these words in such a sense as they might perhaps rightly bear if they had been spoken in a figure or in a parable.

It is sad to think that there are some in our day who do this; they argue thus,—When our LORD says, "*I am the Door,*" or "*I am the Vine,*" He only intends to say, that a Door or a Vine is a figure or a type of Himself in some respect or other. So, when He says, "*This is My Body,*" He only intends to say, "*This Bread is a figure or type of My Body.*"

But in answer to this reasoning, it must be said that our LORD in those other cases was confessedly speaking in a Figure or Parable, but that in the case before us He is not doing so, but He is solemnly and with His dying breath instituting a positive Ordinance to be the distinguishing Rite of His Religion to the end of time, and that therefore we have no liberty at all allowed us to interpret His Words as if they had been spoken in a parable or in a figure.

Besides, if all that our LORD meant was, "*This is a figure of My Body,*" then, at once, we must confess that the One distinctive Rite of the Christian Religion is simply and only on a level with the Jewish Rites of old, it is no better than they were, it is a Rite of the very same kind. For when they offered a slain Sacrifice, they might have truly said, "*This is a figure or type of the slain Sacrifice which is coming. This body of a bleeding suffering dying lamb sets forth before my faith the Body of the very Lamb of God offered on the Cross.*" That Jewish Rite was a figure of something absent, it was a type of something future. So, if we interpret our LORD's Words "*This is My Body*," as if they were "*This is a figure of My Body*," we have the same kind of Rite still; nothing higher or better: all we can say is, "*This is a figure of the absent Body of the Lord;*" or, "*By this broken Bread I set forth to my faith the Sacrifice of the Lord's Death.*"

If this be all, we might almost be inclined to envy those Jews who had in a bleeding dying lamb so much more lively and impressive a figure of the Death of the Lamb of GOD than we have in merely broken Bread and poured out Wine.

And yet, as we must further urge against this figurative interpretation, at the very moment of the Institution of the Eucharist, our LORD was confessedly beginning to put an end to all types and shadows, He was beginning to change the shadow into the Substance, the figure into the Reality, the type into the Antitype.

How then can it be that the one only distinctive Rite of the Church of CHRIST is nothing higher or better than the former Jewish Rites; still, only a figure of something absent, only a shadow of something past? How can we believe that at the Institution of the Holy Eucharist our LORD only put one figure into the place of another?

But, lastly, inasmuch as to contend that our LORD only meant to say, "*This is a figure of My Body*," really changes His Words "*This is My Body*," into "*This is not My Body*," it is quite impossible to admit this modern interpretation. We cannot but firmly hold that our LORD chose the most exact language, and that He *meant* with absolute precision what He *said* when He spoke the words, "*This is My Body*."

Others change the word "*is*" into "*shall be.*" As if our LORD meant, "*This Bread, which I have now blessed and broken, shall be to you who properly receive it My Body.*" But if our LORD had meant this, we may humbly rest satisfied that He would have taken due care to express such meaning with sufficient accuracy. Until we are at liberty to change our LORD's Words, surely we must not venture to alter "*is*" into "*shall be.*" We cannot believe that there is the slightest inaccuracy in the words of this Divine Saying. We must receive and believe it, just as it is. Our LORD did not use the present tense when He should have used the future tense.

And our LORD, as He is GOD, is able to make good His own Words.

So that we must understand and believe that in the Holy Eucharist there is the true and real Presence of the Body of CHRIST, in some heavenly manner, in some holy Mystery. This indeed it is which makes the tremendous greatness of this Divine Institution.

For as one of our Homilies well expresses it, "*Thus much we must be sure to hold, that in the Supper of the Lord there is no vain ceremony, no bare sign, no untrue figure of a thing absent.*" Rather the Thing signified by the outward Sign is present, not absent. The outward part of the Holy Sacrament is a Sign, not of the absence, but of the presence of the LORD's Body. A Jewish Service had the figure, or sign, or type only, the reality was absent and future. But a Christian Sacrament consists of two parts, one outward and visible, the other inward and invisible; one natural and earthly, the other supernatural and spiritual; and here, one is the broken and consecrated Bread, the other is the Body of CHRIST; and both parts are present; each one according to its own nature and substance. If either of the two essential parts of the Sacrament were absent, the Sacrament would no longer be a Sacrament. Here therefore is the tremendous greatness of the Sacrament; not only is there in it the Bread which we break, but as well the very Body of the Incarnate LORD. Thus much we must most firmly hold, resting our faith entirely and simply on our LORD's own Words, "*This is My Body ;*" which words we dare not alter in the very slightest particular.

But this fundamental doctrine of the Real Presence of the LORD's Body in this Holy Sacrament is so great a one, that we must carefully consider some further particulars relating to it in some succeeding chapters.

III. "*Which is given for you.*"
This should be more exactly translated thus: "*which is being given for you;*" because the word "*given*" is in the original language a *present* participle, distinctly denoting an action not past, nor future, but present. We may not change the significance of this word. It distinctly denotes something now present. We cannot believe that our LORD would have used one tense, but meant another.

And this word "*given*" here bears an intensely *sacrificial* sense. For *given to the Apostles* and *given for them unto God* denote two distinct actions. "*Given for you*" cannot here mean less than "*given in sacrifice.*" For anything that is solemnly given or offered unto GOD is a Sacrifice; and such therefore especially, infinitely indeed above all besides, is "*the offering of the Body of Jesus Christ.*" This is the One only Sacrifice, on account of which all other Offerings ever have been or ever can be made acceptable Sacrifices unto GOD.

Here, then, our Great Redeemer solemnly begins the Sacrifice of Himself; He begins His Priestly Office as the true Melchizedec; He begins to "*give Himself*" as "*an Offering and a Sacrifice to God.*" (Eph. v. 2.) And "*for you*" completes the signification of our LORD's sacrificial Action.

Our LORD, therefore, thus explains His Action by His Word: "*This is My Body, which is now being given, or offered in Sacrifice, to the Father, on your behalf, for your sins.*"

And with like meaning, of course: "*This is My Blood, which is now being shed, in Sacrifice to God, for your sins.*"

That very night, therefore, the very and true Sacrifice began, in a holy Mystery. By that very Action, our LORD presented, or gave, or offered His Body and His Blood, in Sacrifice for our sins, unto GOD the FATHER. His own Words expressly say so. We have nothing to do but to believe them.

The very and true Sacrifice of the Lamb of GOD began that night; it was consummated once for all in Blood and Death on the Cross a few hours afterwards; and then it was carried in and completed and accepted by being presented within the veil by the Great High Priest Himself, its Blood being sprinkled on the true Mercy-Seat above, for continual Propitiation for the sins of the world.

The four Holy Writers who relate the Institution of the Eucharist all assure us that our LORD said "*is given*" and "*is shed*," not "*shall be*." So that we cannot be so bold as to change the tense. The One Oblation of Himself was then truly begun. Then followed the actual death on the Cross; and then the Oblation of the all-atoning Blood within the veil. It is all One Action; and it was begun at that Holy Eucharist. There is no more difficulty in holding this Eucharistic Sacrifice before the actual Death on the Cross, than in holding the necessary truth that the Priestly Action of our LORD in the Oblation of Himself was not finished before He entered into the true Holy of Holies "*with His own Blood*." On the Cross our LORD did not *give Himself* as the true Priest after the Order of Melchizedec, but at the Eucharist He did. There with or under the Elements of Bread and Wine He gave His Body and Blood, even Himself, in sacrifice, unto GOD the FATHER, for us.

IV. "*Take, eat :*" "*Drink ye all of this.*"

Our LORD, having first offered or "*given*" His Body and His Blood, in heavenly truth and mystery, in sacrifice "*for us*" unto the FATHER, then proceeds to give these Divine Gifts unto His Disciples, for their Spiritual Food and Sustenance unto Eternal Life in Him. His words, "*Take, eat,*" and "*Drink ye all of this,*" would bring to their minds, if not at that moment, yet certainly afterwards, what the LORD had before said to them concerning their reception of His Body and of His Blood. As Jews, also, accustomed to the rites of Sacrifice from their youth, they would be sure to understand these words in connection with what those former Rites had all along so expressly taught, namely, that the Sacrifice was *to be partaken of* by the offerers of it. In the case of the Paschal Lamb, the idea of partaking of its sacrificed body was a most essential one; as it was also in so many other Sacrifices, in which a Feast upon the Sacrifice had all along been Divinely foreordained; foreshadowing the present infinite Reality that in the Holy Eucharist the Body and the Blood of CHRIST, our true Paschal Lamb, are first of all "*given*" in Sacrifice to GOD, and then given to us for a most Holy and Heavenly Communion, that we may be made partakers of the Sacrifice. For these were *two* most distinct Actions of our LORD: *first*, to give Himself to the FATHER in Sacrifice for us, and *then* to give Himself to us, in a most Holy Communion.

V. "*This Cup is the New Testament in My Blood.*"
Here it is certain that the original word, which is translated *Testament*, would be much better translated by the word *Covenant*, as it is in so many other places where it is used, for instance in Heb. viii. 6, "*The Mediator of a better Covenant.*"

These words, therefore, "*This Cup is the New Covenant in My Blood,*" can only be rightly understood by persons acquainted with the Rites of the Old Covenant. Our LORD's words here expressly refer us to the Old Covenant. We are evidently obliged at once to say, "*What then was the Cup of the Old Covenant,*" with which our LORD here contrasts "*the Cup of the New Covenant ?*" It is plain that we ought to make ourselves acquainted with the ordinances of the Old Covenant, before we can fully enter into these words of our LORD.

Let us, then, call to mind that part of the history of GOD's people of old which S. Paul relates in Heb. xii. When the Israelites had been redeemed out of Egypt, and had arrived at Mount Sinai, it pleased GOD to appoint a solemn Occasion on which His peculiar Covenant with them should be made in the most distinct and impressive manner. (Exod. xxiv.) The dreadful Glory of the Divine Presence abode on the holy Mount; Moses was the Mediator of that Covenant, and all the people stood below. An Altar was built, and Sacrifices slain. "*And Moses took half of the Blood and put it in basons; and half of the Blood he sprinkled on the Altar. And he took the Book of the Covenant, and read in the audience of the people; and they said, All that the Lord hath said will we do, and be obedient. And Moses took the Blood, and sprinkled it on the people, and said, Behold the Blood of the Covenant, which the Lord hath made with you.*"

In contrast with this, S. Paul writes that we Christians are come *to Jesus, the Mediator of the New Covenant, and to the true Blood of sprinkling.*

That former Blood of sprinkling was for the Israel of old, it was the Blood of the Old Covenant; but now to us Christians, the LORD JESUS, the Mediator of a better Covenant, says, in the Holy Eucharist, "*This is the Blood of the New Covenant,*" or, "*This is the New Covenant in My Blood;*" that is, This is the sealing with you of the New Covenant of Grace and Life which has now been established between GOD and His redeemed people, through the Sacrifice of My Blood. For our LORD *repeats the words of Moses of old,* only with infinitely deeper truth and reality.

And if we look back upon all the ancient Sacrifices of the old world, as well as upon the Jewish Sacrifices, our SAVIOUR's Words evidently carry with them as much meaning as this: "This Cup is the great

Rite of the New Covenant which is established between GOD and man through My Sacrifice. The bloody Sacrifices of former ages, with their offerings of bread and wine, were the Rites of the Old Covenant, this now succeeds to them, and comprehends the Reality which they only prefigured. The Old Covenant was contracted with the blood of bulls and of goats; this New Covenant with Mine."

Here also let us call to mind how often GOD has condescended to human infirmity, by giving us not only Promises, but as well *Seals* of those Promises. How often has it pleased GOD to establish some Covenant with man, and at the same time to appoint some Seal, some visible Pledge or Token of that Covenant, for the assistance of our weak faith, for the confirmation of our hope in His Word.

For instance, when, after the Deluge, GOD established a Covenant with the world, He was pleased at the same time to appoint the Rainbow to be the visible Seal of that Covenant, the visible Pledge of the truth of His Promise, saying, " *This is the Token of the Covenant.*" (Gen. ix.)

The same kind of condescension to human infirmity we find in the case of Abraham, Gen. xv. It seemed that the Word or Promise of GOD by itself was not sufficient to assure Abraham's faith; for he asked for *some Sign,* he desired some present Token, some visible Pledge or Seal of the Promise; saying, " *Lord God, whereby shall I know that I shall inherit it?*" So it pleased GOD to give him a visible Sign to be the Pledge and Seal of His Promise, to confirm and assure his faith.

The same we may also see in the case of Gideon, Judges vi. 17; and in the case of Hezekiah, 2 Kings xx. 8; and of Zacharias, S. Luke i. 18.

In all these cases we read that GOD granted to His servants visible Seals, present Signs, as Pledges to their very senses, to assure their faith in His Word.

So also, for *all* the members of the Jewish Church,

the Seal and Token of GOD's special Covenant with them was the Rite or Sign of Circumcision. (Gen. xvii. 9, 10, 13.)

And now for us, in the Church of CHRIST; one of the great purposes for which the Holy Sacraments have been instituted is this very thing, that they should be *visible present standing Seals* of that Great Covenant of Grace which GOD has made with us through Him, Who is "*the Mediator of this better Covenant.*" (Heb. viii. 6.)

The Sacraments are now the Holy Rites and Mysteries, instituted by the SON of GOD when manifest here below in the flesh, for the very purpose of sealing and confirming and renewing, from time to time, the New Covenant of Grace made between GOD and man through the all-atoning Blood of the Sacrifice of His SON.

In the *first* great Sacrament of the Gospel we are *admitted* into this New Covenant of Grace and Life.

In the *second*, this New Covenant is *confirmed and renewed and sealed afresh*, from time to time.

That this is one purpose for which the Holy Sacrament of the Body and Blood of CHRIST has been ordained, is plainly taught us by our LORD's own Words, "*This is My Blood of the New Covenant.*"

Herein, therefore, the New Covenant of Grace is expressly renewed and sealed with each individual who worthily receives this sacred Cup. Here we actually come to the very and true "*Blood of sprinkling.*" (Heb. xii. 24.)

For the precious Blood of the Lamb of GOD is the very Divine Sacrifice itself; for "*the Blood is the Life;*" and if we are made partakers of that Blood, the Covenant is sealed with us individually. If we are made partakers of the Feast upon the Sacrifice, we are necessarily made partakers of the Covenant which is established upon that Sacrifice. The Benefits of the Covenant are sealed to us.

In this greatest of all Sacraments, therefore, it is

verily and indeed said to us, "*Behold the Blood of the Covenant which the Lord hath made with you.*" Here is a visible present and standing Seal of the Covenant of Life in the Blood of CHRIST.

If we come, therefore, in true Repentance and Faith, to this holy Sacrament, we receive, each one for himself, the visible Seal and Pledge of our SAVIOUR'S Love and of GOD'S pardoning Mercy and Grace. For not once only, but "*as often as ye drink this Cup,*" it is the Blood of the LORD, the very Covenant of Grace and Life between GOD and man.

O what a merciful consideration of our fears and our wants; to provide for us a visible pledge of Divine Love, a visible means of taking Him Who is our Life into our inmost being.

Here is comfort of hope and assurance of faith for every worthy receiver. For here we take into our own hands, each one for himself, that *very Seal* of the Covenant of Grace which has been appointed by the LORD Himself.

This is thus ordained that it may be for the exceeding great assurance of our faith and hope. For, if we say, like Abraham of old, "*I hear the general Promises of the Gospel; but, O Lord God, whereby shall I know that they are mine?*" the LORD Himself provides the answer, by putting into our hands this Cup, and saying, "*This Cup is the New Covenant in My Blood. This very Cup, which I now put into your hand, contains, not the Blood of the Old Covenant,* [*which was the blood of bulls and of goats,*] *but My Blood, even the Blood of the New Covenant; by partaking of which you are made a partaker of the Benefits of that very Sacrifice by which the New Covenant of Grace and Life has been established which is now sealed between you and God at this very moment.*"

There are some ill-instructed persons who try to assure their own faith in the Promises of GOD by other means; by working themselves up into a certain state of feeling, or by some remarkable occurrence, or by some sudden conviction, or even by some strange dream; which they take as Seals or Pledges of GOD's Love specially sent to them. Thus they put unauthorized inventions or fancies of their own into the place of the Ordinances of GOD. They put some private acts of devotion of their own into the place of the great Sacraments of the Gospel.

All this, of course, is liable to much self-delusion. We should rather use such Ordinances and Acts of devotion as are appointed for us by direct Divine authority. It is most plain that GOD alone can appoint anything to be *the real visible Seal* of His own Word. Our LORD alone can give us *that* which is really *the very Seal* of the Covenant of Life, the visible, the public Pledge of His Love, for the assurance of our faith and hope. Self-made assurances are without any true and real value.

VI. "*This do.*"

Whatever our LORD then did, therefore, His Church is empowered and commanded to do also, even till He come again. That Action is to be continually repeated by us. Now our LORD's Action essentially consisted, as we have seen, first, *in giving His Body and Blood* in Sacrifice unto GOD the FATHER *for us;* and then in *giving that Body and Blood* to His Disciples, *for them to partake of.* Here was a Sacrifice, and a Feast upon the Sacrifice, which the disciples, being Jews, thoroughly accustomed to such truths, would of course easily understand.

This, therefore, is to be perpetually repeated; the One Sacrifice is to be continually "*given*" or presented unto GOD in this holy Mystery; and then we are to be made partakers of it. Here is the Eucharistic Sacrifice, and then here is the Holy Communion.

The very word "*do*" in "*This do,*" as it has often been shown, is used in a sacrificial sense, really meaning "*This offer.*" It is the very same word in the original which was used by our LORD, when He said, "*I will keep the Passover at thy house*," (S. Matth. xxvi. 18,) or, as it might therefore have been as well translated, "*I will do the Passover;*" and it is the very same word which S. Paul uses in Heb. xi. 28, "*He kept the Passover,*" meaning, "*He sacrificed the Passover.*" And in the Greek translation of the Old Testament which was then commonly used the same word is *very* frequently used in reference to the Levitical Sacrifices, and is generally translated by our words "*offer*" and "*sacrifice.*"

Besides, in the very sentence before us, "*This do ye as often as ye drink it,*" the construction of the original language is strictly thus: "Do as often as ye drink this," the word *it* not being in the original, and the word *this* equally governed by *drink* and by *do*: so that *do this cup* cannot be less than *offer this cup*.

So that when our LORD said at the conclusion of the Passover Supper, "*This do ye,*" He certainly did not mean, "*This eat ye,*" or "*This drink ye,*" but "*Do as I have done,*" "*Offer this,*" or "*Do this Sacrifice,*" or "*Keep this true Passover.*" As much as to say, "As you offered the Lamb in the Passover in sacrifice, in remembrance of your miraculous Redemption out of Egypt, and then all of you partook of it; so now, till I come again, offer this, in continual remembrance of your Redemption by My Blood. By this means, which I now ordain and command, do ye ever show the Sacrifice of My Death, and ever receive the Holy Communion of My Body and Blood."

VII. "*In remembrance of Me.*"

This word "*remembrance*" is not the best English word that could be found, by which to express the sense of the original. The better word would undoubtedly be "*Memorial,*" and this in a very strict and proper sense. For the original word used here by our LORD is a very peculiar word. It is a word frequently used in the Old Testament, and is such as any Jew would properly understand at the time of our LORD's use of it.

That we also may rightly understand it, we must observe its proper use in the Old Testament. In the second chapter of Leviticus the word is used, three times, of *those parts* of the Offerings which were to be offered by fire on the Altar of GOD, before the offerers partook of the remainders of them.

These portions of the Offerings were called *Memorials* of the Offerings; that is to say, they were *Memorials before God*, not Memorials before Man, of the Sacrifice there offered.

This Memorial indeed carried the whole Sacrifice, and presented it before GOD. This is the proper sense of the word, whenever it is used in reference to the ancient Sacrifices.

For we should particularly consider that the ancient typical Sacrifices were intended primarily to set forth before GOD that One true Sacrifice which was coming, and so to worship Him in union with that One Sacrifice. The great primary intention was to *put God in remembrance*. Just in the same kind of sense as when the Prophet wrote, in the Name of GOD, "*Put Me in remembrance*," (Isa. xliii. 26;) and as GOD also had been pleased to speak of Himself to the world through Noah, "*And the Bow shall be in the cloud; and I will look upon it, that I may remember the everlasting Covenant between God and every living creature.*" (Gen. ix. 16.)

So that the sacrificial word *Memorial* has chief respect to GOD, rather than to man.

And the same sense of it may be seen in its use with reference to the Shew-Bread, and also in reference to Aaron bearing the names of the twelve Tribes on his shoulders, &c., which actions were all done *for a Memorial before the Lord*. (See Exod. xxviii. 12; Lev. xxiv. 7; Numb. x. 10.)

This is the peculiar sacrificial word which our LORD

F

used, when He said, "*Do this, for the Memorial of Me;*" as much as to say, "*Let this now be My Memorial,*" or "*the Memorial of My Sacrifice.*"

The emphatic meaning of the words which are in our translation, "*In remembrance of Me,*" is therefore, not "*to put yourselves in remembrance of Me,*" (for the word *remembrance* would most probably have been in that sense a different word in the original,) but it is, "*for a Memorial of My Sacrifice before God.*"

The true and great meaning is, not that very superficial one which is so prevalent in the present day, "*Eat this bread and drink this wine, to put yourselves in remembrance of Me;*" but it is, "*Offer this, for a Memorial of Me before the Father:*" or, in other words, "As you have seen and heard Me do, so do ye to the end of the world: in the way I have done, so do ye also offer the Sacrifice of My Body and of My Blood, under these Signs of Bread and Wine, for a perpetual Memorial of Me before the FATHER, even till I come again."

In the Holy Eucharist, therefore, it is plain, we offer or present continually the Holy Memorial of the Sacrifice of CHRIST before the FATHER; we repeat, by our LORD's express command, that which He Himself did at the first Eucharist; we present, by means of and in union with His own Priestly Ministrations before the Presence of the FATHER at the Heavenly Altar itself, *that One Sacrifice*, which He offered at the Institution of the Eucharist on that last night, which He finished in Blood and Death on the Cross, which He ever since presents and pleads in Heaven. Every Eucharist to the end of the world is simply a repetition or continuation of that one first Eucharist; it is one and ever the same, although offered and partaken of at ten thousand Altars, in every generation, from the beginning to the end of the Christian Dispensation. It is no new fresh Sacrifice, such as the ancient typical and Jewish ones were; but one and ever the same.

To meet solemnly together for a chief Act of Worship, and only to put ourselves in remembrance of the Sacrifice of CHRIST, is entirely insufficient for the very idea of the Act: but, take the other idea, as here explained, and the Act is as great and as grand as all our wants require.

If even of the alms and prayers of Cornelius it is written that they ascended up "*for a Memorial before God*," (Acts x. 4,) how much more so is this Holy Service our one great and high Memorial, ever carrying up to the Heavenly Altar the one all-atoning Sacrifice, and procuring for us the Blessing of Peace and Life.

THE SPIRITUAL SENSE.

"*The Words that I speak unto you, they are Spirit, and they are Life.*" (S. John vi. 63.)

This saying of our LORD'S teaches us that we must understand the Words which He speaks to us concerning the Holy Communion of His Body and Blood in a heavenly super-natural spiritual sense, not in any carnal gross earthly sense. For this saying was spoken in consequence of the gross misunderstanding of His Words by the people in the synagogue at Capernaum. They said, "*How can this Man give us His flesh to eat?*" They thought only of His natural flesh, such as it was then before them; they took His Words in a wrong and shocking sense. In order, therefore, to correct this gross mistake, our LORD said, "*The flesh profiteth nothing: it is the Spirit that quickeneth. The words that I speak unto you, they are Spirit and they are Life.*"

Mere natural flesh, which is all that they were thinking of, could indeed *profit nothing* in giving them eternal Life. Our LORD'S Words, "*My Flesh is Meat indeed,*" relate to a great Mystery. They are to be understood, not according to the laws and properties of nature, but according to the laws and powers of the Spirit and of Life. They belong, not to that mortal natural Body which was then before those Jews, but to the ascended glorified spiritual Body of our LORD.

For we should particularly mark that our LORD had just referred to His Ascension; He connected the Gifts, of which He was speaking, with His Ascension. He said as much as this: "*Why should you be so surprised at what I am saying, when you will soon see this very Body of Mine ascend up into Heaven?*"

For, as S. Paul writes: "*There is a natural Body, and there is a Spiritual Body.*"

And of the spiritual Body of our ascended and glorified LORD, united as it now is for ever with the very Living Godhead, who of us can pretend to understand the amazing properties and powers?

Thus, then, our LORD corrects the gross carnal sense in which His Words were then taken, and teaches us that we must take them in a spiritual mystical supernatural sense; for they belong to the powers of the Spirit and of Life, not to mere natural flesh and blood.

The Words are very special Words, relating to the Operations of Spirit and of Life; to which our present knowledge does not reach. They are words relating to the powers of that risen ascended glorified Body, which is now united to the Living Godhead, in the Person of the SON; by which, as our LORD here reveals to us, the Spirit quickeneth us with the Power of Eternal Life. They are words which belong to Powers beyond all our bodily senses, beyond all our present feelings, above all our human reason; they relate to the Spirit and to the powers of the world to come, even to the power of Eternal Life.

At the same time, however, that we avoid the gross mistake of those Jews, we must take care to avoid another mistake which is often made in the present day.

For many now fancy that when our LORD says, "*My Words are Spirit, and they are Life,*" He means to teach us that we should understand them only in a *figurative* or *metaphorical* sense, as if indeed our LORD only intended to say that we must *feed on Him by faith,* in order to have eternal Life. They explain the words, "*Except ye eat My Flesh,*" as in reality meaning no more than, "*Except ye believe in Me.*"

But this would make it seem that our LORD had used words concerning a most important matter *in a hurry,* so that He was obliged to explain and withdraw them. This would make it seem that our LORD had used the most singular expression, "*Except ye eat My Flesh,*" when He only intended, "*Except ye believe in Me;*" as if He had not known in perfect Wisdom what were the best human Words to use on such an infinitely great matter.

And then also such persons generally suppose that the word *spiritual* means *figurative;* which is a great mistake. That which is *spiritual* is most *real.* GOD Himself is a Spirit, and yet He is a most real Substance. A spiritual Body is as real a Body as a natural Body.

When our LORD therefore says that we must understand His Words, concerning this Holy Communion of His Body, *according to the Spirit and according to Life;* He only takes away the gross carnal sense of them; He does not withdraw their true real spiritual sense in the least degree. The words, "*The flesh profiteth nothing,*" were spoken merely to remove a gross and ignorant misconception, not in the slightest degree to lessen the infinite Truth of the Heavenly Mystery revealed in the words, "*My Flesh is Meat indeed.*" This saying most surely still remains. All the sayings of the SON of GOD, concerning the Holy Communion of His Body and of His Blood, still remain, in all their perfect precision, in all their Heavenly Truth, in all their absolute certainty, in all their tremendous greatness; only, they are removed from the interpretations of mere natural sense and reason, and shown to belong to a supernatural Mystery, relating to the Powers of the ascended glorified Body of the SON of GOD.

When, therefore, our LORD speaks to us in the Holy Sacrament and says, *"Take; eat: this is My Body,"* we must believe His Words, not in any carnal gross or merely natural sense, but in a heavenly supernatural sense; for they relate to the Powers of Spirit and of Life; they belong to the Presence of the spiritual Body, not of the natural; they relate to our participation, in a most heavenly Mystery, in the Glorified Spiritual Living and Life-giving Body of the SON of GOD; whereby our whole being is quickened with the Power of Eternal Life unto the Glories of an immortal Resurrection.

THE ONE ONLY SACRIFICE ONCE OFFERED.

The great subject on which S. Paul writes in the Epistle to the Hebrews, is the present Priesthood of our LORD. The Apostle proves the superiority of this Priesthood over the Jewish Priesthood by several arguments. For instance, he says that the Jewish Priests were *many*, *" they were many Priests,"* (vii. 23,) *" But this Person, because He continueth ever, hath an unchangeable Priesthood."* He hath no Predecessor, no Successor; He is the One ever-abiding Priest: He *" abideth a Priest continually."*

And again, as *the Person* Who is thus our Great High Priest is One and unchangeable, the one only Priest of His Order; so also is *the Sacrifice* which He offers One and alone for ever.

This One Sacrifice for sins is that which the LORD Himself made, of Himself, when *"He gave Himself for us, an offering and a Sacrifice to God."* (Eph. v. 2.) *" This He did once, when He offered up Himself."* (Heb. vii. 27.) So that we are said to be *" sanctified through the Offering of the Body of Jesus Christ once for all:*" and it is also written that our LORD, " *after He had offered One Sacrifice for sins for ever, sat down on the right hand of God.*"

This One Sacrifice, therefore, which was once made in Blood and Death on the Cross, can never be repeated; nothing can be ever added to its value. It is absolutely One and Alone for ever. All the ancient Sacrifices, whether Patriarchal or Judaical, were called Sacrifices, and were of value before GOD, only because they represented, in type and figure, this One infinite and tremendous Sacrifice of the Incarnate SON of GOD.

But, although this One Sacrifice of the true and very Lamb of GOD was thus only *once* offered in Blood and Death, yet it is clear that this One Sacrifice, only once so offered, may be and is continually efficacious; it is ever the same in its virtue and in its effects, even to the end of the world. It is, as the Apostle expresses it, "*One Sacrifice for ever;*" not a fresh Sacrifice from time to time, as those Jewish typical ones were, but one ever the same.

This One only Sacrifice, therefore, and not another, we ever show forth; this only we ever plead, in the Holy Eucharist, for the same ends and purposes for which our Great High Priest Himself, by means of it, intercedes for us above before the very Mercy-Seat of the FATHER.

But to enter into this great truth more fully, we must consider, first of all, that our Great Priest Himself ever shows and presents and pleads this One Sacrifice for sins on our behalf in Heaven itself.

S. Paul writes, (Heb. viii. 8,) "*Every High Priest is ordained to offer Gifts and Sacrifices; wherefore it is of necessity that this Man have somewhat also to offer.*"

What is the Offering, then, that our LORD Himself now ever offers for us, as our Priest before the FATHER? It is, and can be, only, *the One Sacrifice,* which He made of Himself, ever the same.

If there is no existing Sacrifice to offer, there is no existing Priest; for "*it is of necessity,*" the Apostle writes, that a Priest have "*somewhat to offer.*"

In Heaven above, therefore, our LORD now ever appears, as our ever ministering Priest; appearing before the FATHER, in His human Body; ministering in that very Body which still bears the marks of its Sacrifice upon the Cross. He appears as "*a Lamb as it had been slain.*" (Rev. v. 6.) The One Sacrifice for sins is thus ever shown forth in the Heavenly Sanctuary itself; the very Body that was sacrificed on the Cross standing in the Presence of the FATHER.

Consider also further the express type of this oblation of the One Sacrifice in Heaven itself, which was given and ordained by Divine foreknowledge in the Jewish Dispensation.

What may be most properly called the greatest Type and chief Representation upon earth of the Heavenly Realities of the Messiah's Priesthood, took place in the Jewish Church, once a year, on their Great Day of Atonement. It is described in Lev. xvi.: it is expressly referred to by S. Paul in Heb. ix.; and it is said by him to be now realized and fulfilled by our ascended LORD Himself in His perpetual Priesthood.

It was briefly this: Once a year only the High Priest entered in, within the vail, into the Holy of Holies, and appeared before the Mercy-Seat, which was the Seat of the special Presence of GOD. The animal to be offered by the High Priest in Sacrifice, as a sin-offering, was first of all to be slain in the outer Court of the Temple; its Blood was then to be carried in, by the High Priest, within the vail; and then it was sprinkled before and upon the Mercy-Seat, a cloud of Incense at the same time being made to cover the Mercy-Seat. By this means it was that the Sacrifice was brought into the special Presence of GOD: by this means it was offered within the Holy of Holies; thus it was accepted and completed.

The Fat of the Sacrifice of the sin-offering was indeed burnt on the Altar of Sacrifice, and the Body was carried "*without the camp,*" and there burnt as an unclean thing.

But the chief Offering of this Sacrifice of Atonement was distinctly ordered and intended to be made by the High Priest *within the vail,* before the very Mercy-Seat, in the special Presence of GOD.

And this Offering of this Sacrifice, within the vail, summed up and represented and carried in all the Sacrifices of the whole year. All the daily Sacrifices, and all other Sacrifices, were comprehended in this Great One of the yearly Day of Atonement. On this chief occasion, when alone the High Priest entered in and appeared before the Mercy-Seat of GOD, all the Sacrifices of the year were brought in and presented before GOD. Thus was the Atonement made, "*for all their sins once a year.*"

Now all this was one of the most eminent types and figures of the Heavenly Reality itself. This ancient yearly Service, ordained in every particular by Divine foreknowledge, is now fulfilled in the Kingdom of the Messiah; it is all now accomplished, by the Ascension of our true Priest into the very Presence of the FATHER, where He is now "*the Minister of the Sanctuary and of the true Tabernacle,*" (Heb. viii. 2;) ever discharging His Priestly Office on our behalf; abiding "*a Priest continually.*"

Our Great High Priest, having been slain as the Lamb of GOD upon the Cross in the outer court of this world, has now ascended and gone in within the vail, now appearing in His Priesthood before the true Mercy-Seat of the FATHER, not indeed with the Blood of those ancient and typical Sacrifices, but as S. Paul expressly writes, "*with His own Blood.*" (Heb. ix. 12.)

The ancient Type has been fulfilled; our true Priest has ascended and gone in within the vail; and He has carried in with Him according to the truth of the ancient type, *His own Sacrifice;* which He presents,

in Heavenly reality, before the Mercy-Seat of the FA-
THER, together with the Cloud of Incense, the all-
prevailing pleading of His own Intercessions.

We cannot be deceived or misled by thus inter-
preting the Divinely pre-ordained type.

No truth of Divine Revelation can be more certain
than this; that our true Priest now presents the Blood
of the One Sacrifice, in His heavenly Ministrations,
before the FATHER; or, in other words, He continually
offers His own One Sacrifice of Himself, which He
endured once at Calvary in Blood and death; by which
means He makes continual Intercessions on our behalf.

The perpetual presentation of the One perfect Sacrifice is the ground of the perpetual Intercession.

We dare not venture to say that the Sacrifice on
the Cross was completed and accepted, before it was
carried in within the vail, and presented before the
true Mercy-Seat of the FATHER; for that would be
to destroy the significance of the type, which GOD
Himself had so expressly designed and foreordained
in order to reveal to us this very truth. CHRIST
now fulfils in reality that which the Jewish High
Priest did in figure.

The One Sacrifice, therefore, was begun in holy
mystery in the Eucharist; it was endured in Blood
and Death on the Cross; and it is now presented
within the vail, in Heavenly truth and reality.

Therefore, as S. Paul declares, we have now the true
"*sprinkling of Blood,*" even upon the Heavenly Altar.

We dare not venture to say that the Sacrifice on the
Cross was sufficient for our Salvation without the continual Intercession within the vail also.

The Intercessions render effectual to our Salvation
the Sacrifice of the Cross, for it is written, "*He is able
to save to the uttermost, seeing He ever liveth to make
Intercession.*" (Heb. vii. 25.)

But this "*entering in of our Great High Priest within
the vail with His own Blood,*" does not interfere in the

slightest degree with the Oneness of His Sacrifice. It is no new Sacrifice that He presents, but the one Sacrifice, ever the same.

For as there is *One only Priest* for ever, even so there is *One only Sacrifice* for ever. As S. Paul writes, (Heb. x. 12,) "*This Man, after He had offered One Sacrifice for sins for ever, sat down at the right Hand of God.*"

There is therefore now only " *One Sacrifice for sins for ever*." It is this One perpetual Sacrifice which our One true Priest ever presents and pleads before the FATHER; by which means He ever makes intercession for us, and takes away our sins.

And it is exactly *the same One Sacrifice for sins* which by our LORD's own command, and in His own appointed way, His Church on earth also ever shows forth.

There is no new Sacrifice, no repetition of the One Sacrifice, no addition to it,—but a continual showing of it, a continual presentation and pleading of it in the Holy Eucharist before GOD.

This surely does not detract from the Oneness of the Sacrifice; nor does it oppose or contradict anything that S. Paul writes in his Epistle to the Hebrews as to the One Sacrifice being only *once* offered. He is there contrasting the *many* and *repeated* and *fresh* sacrifices of the Jewish Church with the One only Sacrifice which our true Priest endured on the Cross, and ever presents in Heaven. Those Jewish Priests offered continually *fresh* sacrifices every day; but now only One Sacrifice is offered, ever the same, ever one, whether presented in Heaven above by the Great High Priest of the Church Himself in His own Person before the very Presence of the FATHER, or presented on ten thousand altars here below by the hands of those whom He has Himself commissioned for that very purpose.

The Altars are all one; the Sacrifice is all one; the True Priest Himself continually presents all in one at the Heavenly Altar, in heavenly and tremendous reality; for with GOD all is ever present as one.

Our one Priest does, in truth and reality, continually show forth and present the One eternal Sacrifice, Himself, both above and below. Thus it is all one Service, one Worship, above and below; one continual showing forth of the one only Sacrifice for sins.

By this means the Worship of the Church on earth is identified with the Ministration of our Great High Priest in the true Sanctuary above.

In the Sacrifice of old, we might very properly distinguish *three* parts.

There was, first, the devotion of the animal to sacrifice, in will and in intention on the part of the Offerer.

Then there was the actual death at the Altar of GOD.

Then there was the solemn presentation of the Blood of the Sacrifice before the special Presence of GOD by the High Priest.

All these *three* parts however formed but *one* Sacrifice; they were not *three* Sacrifices, but only *one* Sacrifice.

The same distinction may be made with regard to the Antitype itself.

The Sacrifice which we offer in the Eucharist is not a repetition of the Bloody Sacrifice offered on the Cross, but it is a repetition of the Unbloody Sacrifice offered at the first Institution of the Eucharist, when the Priesthood of the order of Aaron came to an end, and the Priesthood of the order of Melchizedec began. The Eucharistic Sacrifice remains in all ages of the Church *that* which it was in that very night when our Great High Priest first offered it.

That which our Divine Priest is Himself ever doing for us before GOD in Heaven above, and that which He does for us here below, as our true Melchizedec at His earthly Altar, are both one, in spiritual reality; it is all one continual presenting of CHRIST Himself as the Lamb slain to take away our sins.

Hence, S. Chrysostom writes: "*There, on the Altar, lies the common expiation of the world; when the people stand with uplifted hands, a Priestly Assembly, and that awful Sacrifice lies displayed, how shall we not prevail with God by our entreaties?*"

And S. Ambrose: "*Christ is offered upon earth, when the Body of Christ is offered.*"

And our own Bishop Taylor: "*The Church is the image of heaven, the Priest the minister of Christ, the holy Table a copy of the celestial Altar, and the eternal Sacrifice of the Lamb, slain from the beginning of the world, is always the same. It bleeds no more after the finishing of it upon the Cross; but it is wonderfully represented in heaven, and graciously represented here; by Christ's action there, by His commandment here.*"

And Bishop Overall: "*This is no new Sacrifice, but the same which was once offered, and which is every day offered to God by Christ in heaven; and the Church intends not to have any new Propitiation or remission of sins obtained, but to make that effectual, and in act applied unto us, which was once obtained by the Sacrifice of Christ on the Cross.*"

And Archbishop Bramhall thus sums up the doctrine of the Eucharistic Sacrifice: "*We acknowledge an Eucharistic Sacrifice of praise and thanksgiving; a commemorative Sacrifice, or a Memorial of the Sacrifice of the Cross; a representative Sacrifice, or a representation of the Passion of Christ before the eyes of His Father; an impetrative Sacrifice, or an impetration of the fruit of His Passion, by way of real prayer; and lastly, an applicative Sacrifice, or an application of His merits to our souls.*"

Thus CHRIST is our Priest *now* ever ministering for us in Heaven. He does not merely pray for us, which is the only idea which some seem to have of His Intercession, just as any good man may intercede for us by praying for us; but our LORD is performing some office of His Priestly Power. His Priesthood is a present reality; it is as really necessary for our Salvation, as His death on the Cross was. He is offering His One Sacrifice within the vail; He is sprinkling the Blood of the One Sacrifice on the true Altar above; and He is covering the very Mercy-Seat of GOD with the cloud of His Intercessions.

And upon earth He is also *continually* a Priest, according to the order of Melchizedec, ministering for us in the Holy Eucharist by the hands and voice of His Priests on earth, for the same ends and according to the same realities as He does in Heaven.

But all is One and the same Sacrifice for ever.

The Sacrifice of the Christian Altar is the very Sacrifice of the Cross, and the offering of it is the Act of the Great High Priest Himself; it is a very special Act of His Priestly Office; it is a very special performance of His Intercession on our behalf, which He never ceases to make.

Some contend that to say that the Offering of the Sacrifice of the Cross is continually made in the Holy Eucharist contradicts or interferes with the truth that the Sacrifice is only one, and only once offered.

But it might as well be objected that the Offering of the Sacrifice within the vail by the Jewish High Priest made that Sacrifice a double Sacrifice.

If it be thought necessary to restrict the One Offering to the actual Death upon the Cross alone, for fear of interfering with the doctrine of the One Sacrifice once offered, then we must as well restrict the whole Sacrifice under the Jewish Law to the act of offering the animal at or upon the outer Altar, and say that the Sacrifice was finished and completed before its Blood was brought in and offered by the High Priest within the Holy of Holies; which is what few perhaps would venture to urge.

So that if this offering of the Sacrifice in Heaven does not cause the Sacrifice to cease to be *one and once offered*, no more of course does the offering of it in the Eucharist upon earth cause it to cease to be *one and once offered*.

The Oneness that the Apostle insists upon is rather only opposed to the continual multiplication of fresh Sacrifices under the Jewish Law, than to the doctrine of the continual presentation of this One Sacrifice ever the same, both above and below, by our One true Priest.

ON THE WORDS "SPIRITUAL," "SUBSTANCE," AND "MYSTERY."

It is very necessary that we should use words in as accurate and exact a sense as possible, when we speak of any Heavenly Mystery. Before we further consider the Divine Words, "*This is My Body*," we ought therefore to consider the proper sense of the words "*spiritual*," and "*substance*," and "*mystery*."

The proper meaning of the word "*substance*" is much deeper than that in which it is commonly used. We commonly use it of any material thing : we call such things as *bread, water, iron,* &c., "*substances*." But when we wish to speak with greater accuracy, we are obliged to make a distinction between the *substance* of anything and the *properties* or *qualities* of that thing ; because we find that the *properties* or *qualities* of the thing may become changed, whilst the *substance* of it remains unchanged. For instance ; if we take into our hands some grains of wheat, we see their colour, we feel their hardness, we smell their smell, we taste their taste. That is to say, the *qualities* or *properties* of the grains become known to us through our bodily senses.

But now let us have these grains of wheat ground into flour. Then we find that their hardness, their smell, their appearance, their taste, are all changed. But yet the *substance* of the grains remains still the same. The *qualities* or *properties* are changed, but not the *essential substance*.

Then again if we make the flour into bread, what a

change takes place in their *properties* and *qualities*, whilst we believe the *essential substance* is still the same as before.

Or, to take another example: how greatly do the properties of wax become altered, when we subject it to the influence of fire. Where is the wax candle which is burnt up by the flame? Its substance is not annihilated, but remains still, although invisible and under very altered conditions.

And again, when we evaporate water, or turn it into steam, by heat, and make it invisible, how greatly are its properties changed, its real and essential substance still remaining.

By such examples as these we may be assisted perhaps in some degree to understand that a thing may be very much changed in all those qualities or properties of it which our senses are able to perceive, and yet that the *essence* or *substance* of that thing may remain unchanged.

For by *substance* we properly mean that *essence* of a thing which causes it to be that thing and to have such and such properties or powers of affecting our senses.

So, when we talk of sugar being sweet, we simply mean that sugar is a thing of such a substance as has the power or property of exciting in our palate the sensation of sweetness.

But what the *essential substance* of anything is in itself, we know not. It is beyond the reach of our senses, and above the limits of our present knowledge. We know what a thing is, only by those *properties* or *qualities* of it which our senses can perceive; but not by its *essence* or *substance*.

The word *substance* cannot therefore be limited in its proper use to things made of earthly materials. It is a word which may be used by us, for want of a better one, with reference to *all things that exist*, even including the Divine Being Himself. All things that exist, it is plain, must have some *substance* or *essence*, or they are nothing at all. Angels must have some kind of substance, though we may call it a *spiritual substance*, to distinguish it from the substance of any earthly thing. GOD Himself is a Spirit, the One only self-existing Spirit, and yet we are not able to conceive of His existence apart from the possession of some spiritual essence or Substance. So that we confess, in our Creeds, that our LORD JESUS CHRIST is in His Divine Nature, "*of one Substance with the Father;*" and we hold the co-existence of Three Persons in One Godhead, "*neither confounding the Persons nor dividing the Substance;*" and also, we believe, concerning the Nature of the SAVIOUR of the World, that He is, "*God, of the substance of the Father, and Man of the substance of His Mother.*"

By "*substance*" therefore we do not mean anything of necessity made of earthly matter. It is used alike of things animate and things inanimate, of things earthly and things heavenly. It is used to express that which is the very principle of the being or of the life of anything, without which it would not be that thing. But it is a word which rather expresses our ignorance than our knowledge. As yet we have no knowledge at all concerning the Substances of things, but only concerning their qualities or properties.

So that no human mind is able to draw any line of distinction between material and spiritual Substances. We cannot define Matter, or Spirit, with any human words. Our knowledge does not reach as yet to that which is the Essence or Substance of anything. The Laws which belong to Heavenly or Spiritual Substances are as yet unknown to us.

Next, as to the proper sense of the word "*Spiritual.*" We often use it in a popular and loose kind of way, as if it were the same in sense as the word "*figurative*" or "*metaphorical.*" But this is not the true and accurate meaning of the word. If we use it with accuracy, we must use it to express *that which belongs to the spirit*, in distinction to *that which belongs to the flesh*. Just as "*sensual*" properly expresses that which belongs to the *senses*, and "*carnal*" that which belongs to the *flesh*, so "*spiritual*" means that which belongs to the *spirit*.

So that when we speak accurately of our "*spiritual food and sustenance*," we do not mean to speak of a *mere figurative* or *metaphorical* Food, but of a Food which properly belongs to the Sustenance of the Life of our Spirit. Earthly food, such as bread and wine, the fruits of the earth, constitute our *bodily sustenance*, but the Body and Blood of CHRIST are said in Holy Scripture to constitute our *spiritual food*, that is, food for the sustenance of the Life of our Spirit: for every existing Life requires some food or sustenance from without itself, except of course the One Self-existing Life.

Again, the word "*spiritually*" is used in distinction from the word "*carnally*," when it is said that we "*spiritually eat the Flesh of Christ.*" It is no mere eating such as when we eat our natural earthly food, but it is a *spiritual eating*, because it is a Heavenly Mystery; it belongs to the Spirit, not to the flesh; it is not a mere *carnal eating*, but a *spiritual eating*.

But here we must bear in mind that that which is *spiritual* is just as *real* and *true* as that which is *carnal*. A Spiritual or Heavenly Substance is just as *true* and as *real* a Substance, as a carnal or earthly substance.

Our LORD speaking of our reception of His Body and of His Blood, says, "*My Flesh is the true Meat, and My Blood is the true Drink;*" although it is *spiritual* Food, yet it is *true* and *real;* and the action of receiving it is a true and real action, although it must rather be called a *spiritual* action than a *carnal* one, inasmuch as in its chief and infinite greatness it belongs to the laws and powers of the spirit.

It is also necessary that we here consider the statement made by S. Paul; "*There is a natural body, and there is a spiritual body.*" Our present body he calls "*a natural body:*" the body which we shall have after the Resurrection he calls "*a spiritual body.*" The word *spiritual* is therefore used by the Apostle in distinction from *natural*. But it is not used by him, in the slightest degree, in the sense of "*figurative.*" The spiritual body is just as *true* and as *real* a body as the natural body is. It will be indeed the very *same* body, in essential substance, as before; but its properties and qualities may become so changed after the Resurrection from the dead, that it can no longer be called a *natural* body, but rather a *spiritual* body. The word *spiritual*, as here used, means therefore plainly the same as *supernatural*, or the same as the word "*heavenly*" as used by S. Paul when in the same passage of his Epistle he writes, "*As is the Heavenly Adam, such are they also that are heavenly :*" for our bodies at the Resurrection will be fashioned anew, they will be made like unto the Spiritual Body of the Second Adam.

The word "*Mystery*" properly signifies some truth revealed to us which contains in it that which reaches far above and beyond our present knowledge.—As when S. Paul writes, "*Great is the Mystery of Godliness, God was manifest in the flesh ;*" here is a truth revealed unto us, that GOD was manifested here upon earth in our flesh, the Word was made flesh; but in this truth there is that which completely transcends our present knowledge.

When again we speak of the Church as the Mystical Body of CHRIST, the word mystical is used to signify that although we know by Revelation that the Church is now so constituted in CHRIST as to be His Body, yet there is in this revealed truth that which is quite above and beyond our knowledge; for we know not the manner of the union which subsists between the Head and the members of this Body.

In like manner we call the doctrine of the Holy Trinity a Mystery: and so on.

The word *mystery* or *mystical* does not at all imply that the thing spoken of is a mere figure or metaphor or parable.

THE REAL PRESENCE.

By simple and unquestioning faith in our LORD'S own most express and solemn Words, "*This is My Body*," we learn to believe, that, when these Divine Words have been pronounced, according to the express Institution and Commandment of our LORD, then He makes good His own Words, He causes the spiritual substance of His own Body to be present, in or with or under the vail of the visible and outward sign.

So that then *both* Parts of the Holy Sacrament are present, namely, the outward and visible Part, that is, natural Bread; and also, the inward and invisible Part, that is, the Body of CHRIST. The outward visible Part then becomes the Divinely ordained Sign and Pledge of the Presence of the inward invisible Part. It is then a Sign, given to our very senses, to assure our faith, not of the absence but of the presence of the LORD'S Body.

And in like manner we learn to believe in the real Presence of the Blood of CHRIST.

This Presence of the Body of CHRIST in the holy Sacrament is a *spiritual* Presence, that is to say, it is a Presence not according to the laws of the presence of earthly or carnal bodies, but it is according to the laws of a Spiritual Body. It is a *real* Presence although *spiritual*. It is a Presence supernatural and heavenly, altogether above and beyond the reach of our present knowledge. The mode or manner in which the Spiritual Substance of our LORD'S Body becomes present with the earthly substance of the consecrated

Bread, is altogether beyond the limits of our knowledge.

But the absolute truth of the fact we must firmly believe, on the simple authority of our LORD's own Words, "*This is My Body.*" For these are Words of the utmost possible precision and exactness.

To our bodily senses, therefore, we may say, "*This is Bread;*" but to our faith, "*This is the Body of Christ.*"

We believe that both parts of the Sacrament are truly, really, substantially present; the *one* according to the laws and powers of the kingdom of nature, *the other* according to the laws and powers of the kingdom of Grace.

There is no contradiction of one against the other; no interference of one with the other.

Our senses do not deceive us when they inform us that in the Holy Sacrament we eat Bread and drink Wine; but neither can our faith deceive us, when it informs us, on the authority of our LORD's own Words, that we receive, *verily and indeed,* the Body and Blood of CHRIST.

Here it may perhaps serve to help our faith in this great Article of the Christian Revelation, if we consider that our LORD's Body is now a Spiritual Body, and that therefore It is raised above all the laws and conditions of a mere earthly natural body. Moreover we must bear in mind, that It is united for ever to the Living Godhead; so that Its Powers are Powers of Life and of Spirit altogether above and beyond our knowledge. It is, verily and indeed, the Body of GOD.

What difficulty, therefore, can there be in believing that our LORD being GOD is able to make His Body to be present in any special manner that He pleases, and under any condition that He is pleased to appoint? Surely the special supernatural Presence of this Spiritual Body in the Holy Eucharist is a Mystery of our Faith not greater or more difficult to receive than many others which we firmly hold.

Perhaps we may be further assisted in receiving this Mystery, if we may be permitted to take some illustrations from the Kingdom of Nature; for "*all things are double, one against another;*" so that by the analogies of Natural Laws, we are often assisted in perceiving the Mysteries of the Kingdom of Heaven.

If we take a piece of glass, *light* may be made to be *present in it,* or absent from it, according to our pleasure.

If we take a piece of iron, we may cause *heat* to be communicated into it, so as to be *present in it,* and to penetrate its whole mass. And if we could find a person who did not know what *heat* is, we might put this piece of heated iron into his hand, and say, "*This is heat.*"

We can also cause the *electric fluid* to be present in the telegraphic wire, and we can communicate its presence from one end of the world to another in a wonderfully short time.

In our own selves, the Presence of the living Soul is the life of every part of our own Body, even of the most remote member. Here is an instance of one Substance, and that a Spiritual one, being in another Substance, and that a carnal one. For "*the reasonable Soul and Flesh is one Man.*" But there is no confusion or interference of Substance one with the other, although in this instance one affects the other in the most powerful manner.

In the case of the Burning Bush, Moses beheld in it not only the unconsumed natural Bush, but as well the burning Glory of the Divine Presence. It was a great Miracle to all appearance; but if we consider it, it does not perhaps at all follow that the fiery glory of the Divine Presence in the Bush was of such a nature as to make it consume any earthly matter. The Presence of the Bush in its natural substance was most probably entirely unaffected by the special Presence of God in it; for *one* Presence was an earthly natural Presence, the other was a spiritual and Divine Presence. The two co-existed, neither interfering with the other.

Another illustration we may take from one of the Mysteries of the Kingdom of CHRIST. For the Real Presence of the LORD's Body in the Holy Eucharist is very like the Mystery of the Divine Incarnation. "*The Word was made Flesh,*" and yet the Word remained the same. His Divine Nature was unchanged by His Incarnation. They beheld the LORD Incarnate living as Man amongst themselves; they looked upon Him, they heard Him, they touched Him; and to all their senses He was Man. Yet although they beheld His Manhood only, they saw One Who was GOD. They who touched the Flesh of CHRIST, touched GOD, and yet GOD is not Flesh; but GOD was present in that Flesh. To their bodily senses, He was Man; to their faith, He was GOD.

Even so, in the Holy Eucharist, there is present to the bodily senses only Bread, but in or with or beneath the vail of that Bread there is the Presence of the Body of CHRIST.

This is the truth which makes all the tremendous greatness of the holy Sacrament. Here the spiritual Substance of the very and true Body of GOD Incarnate is caused to be present by the Power of the Eternal Spirit, in a most profound Mystery, in a supernatural manner. This, we may say, is a Miracle indeed, greater than all Miracles. This is the standing Miracle of the Christian dispensation.

Here we should consider a moment some truths relating to the Divine Presence. Although in some true sense GOD is ever in Heaven above, yet we believe in His Omnipresence. His Presence is not restricted by time or space. And yet this Presence of GOD may be revealed or manifested in some way, at some special time, or in some special place, more than at another, for some special purpose; as it was occasionally to the Patriarchs of old, and as it was on the Mercy-Seat in the Jewish Temple.

In Paradise, our first Parents "*hid themselves from the Presence of the Lord.*" And it is also written that Cain "*went out from the Presence of the Lord.*" To Moses GOD said, "*My Presence shall go with thee.*" Of the Mercy-Seat it was promised, "*There I will meet with thee.*" And again it is written, "*The Lord came down in a cloud.*" And at the dedication of Solomon's Temple, "*The Glory of the Lord filled the House of the Lord.*"

So that we plainly learn that a special Presence of GOD is not inconsistent with His Omnipresence.

When the Second Person of the Godhead came down to this world, His Presence here below was such that He was not absent from Heaven above. He remained still present there, as He especially declared to Nicodemus. (S. John iii. 13.)

And although now He has ascended in His human Body, yet He is still present here below, according to His own Promise, "*Lo, I am with you always, even to the end of the world.*"

Notwithstanding the ever abiding Presence of our LORD's Body at the right hand of the FATHER, yet we cannot say that that Body is absent from any place where He Himself is; for the Manhood and the Godhead are in Him now for ever united. His human Body is now inseparable from His Divinity. The Presence of His Body is now therefore extended, in some true and real manner, in some heavenly Mystery, throughout the whole Church; as S. Paul teaches us by calling the Church, since the Ascension, "*The Fulness of Him Who filleth all in all,*" (Eph. i. 23;) for He ascended in the Body for this very purpose, that no longer as GOD only, but as Man also, "*He might fill all things,*" with His Presence. (Eph. iv. 10.)

This Presence of the LORD Incarnate is therefore now one of the great Mysteries of our Christian Faith. He is present, in some special way, throughout the whole Church, which is His Body, both in His Human and in His Divine Nature.

This Presence, not being according to the laws of mere earthly things, is not perceptible by any of our bodily senses. We know it only by Faith.

It is not inconsistent with this universal Presence of our LORD in the Church, that He should grant His Presence in some special manner, at some special times, for some special purposes, in some special places.

A most special Presence of our LORD, it is plain, is granted us in the Holy Eucharist at our Christian Altars; for here He says to us most expressly, "*This is My Body;*" and we must ever bear in mind that the Presence of our LORD Himself cannot be separated from the Presence of His Body.

And here we should also consider that the Presence of the LORD's Body in the Holy Eucharist is, not the Presence of His dead Body, but the Presence of His Living Body. It is not a bare remembrance of His Body dead upon the Cross which we here make, but it is rather the Presence of His Living Body which we adore, and worship, and receive.

For we must consider that each holy Eucharist is still the same in its Nature as the very first one was. When our LORD said at the first one, "*This is My Body,*" He then caused to be present that same Body which He causes to be present still in every holy Eucharist. For our LORD had not, nor has two Bodies, but only one, from the beginning of His Incarnation for ever. And at that first Eucharist, it is plain, our LORD did not speak of His natural Body as it was then visibly present in its mere carnal and mortal state, nor did He speak of His Body as it was when crucified and dead upon the Cross; but of necessity, when He said of That which was in His hand, "*This is My Body,*" He spoke of the very essential Principle, the real Substance of His Body, invisible, transcending all our knowledge, which He as GOD can cause to be present where and how He pleases.

It is the Presence of the true and real and essential Substance of His Body, which is now an ascended and glorified Body, raised above all the laws of mere natural and earthly substances.

Moreover, as this Body is the very Body of GOD Incarnate, it is Life-giving; and it is caused to be specially present here, in order that we should be made partakers of It for the sustenance of our very Life in CHRIST, as we shall consider more particularly in another chapter.

We should also here call to mind what is related to us concerning our LORD's Body after it was raised from the dead and made a Spiritual Body. We read that It was visible to the senses, or invisible, according to the pleasure of our LORD; and that It could pass through a closed door. So that we learn that an earthly substance opposed no hindrance to the passage of our LORD's Body from one place to another. And we need not believe that the earthly substance of that door was at all changed, or even affected in the slightest manner by the passage of the LORD's Spiritual Body through it.

What powers the risen spiritual Body of our LORD may have received on its Ascension into the Glory of the FATHER we do not know. But we must bear in mind that it is now the glorified Body of GOD the SON; it cannot be separated from the Godhead; its Powers must be altogether beyond our conception; it is both Living and Life-giving.

Lastly, we should consider that we all firmly believe that our LORD is able to be present in ten thousand Assemblies of the Church upon earth at the same moment, ever making good His own Words, "*Where two or three are gathered together in My Name, there am I in the midst.*" This we all undoubtingly believe.

And as our LORD is inseparably both Man as well as GOD, His Manhood cannot be absent where His Godhead is present. So that our LORD's Body, we believe, is really and truly present wherever He Himself is present.

There can therefore be no reasonable difficulty in believing that our LORD can cause His Body to be present in a holy Mystery on ten thousand Altars at the same moment, whenever those conditions are fulfilled which He has made necessary for that special sacramental Presence.

If our LORD can be present with every Believer at the same moment throughout the whole Church, caring for every one just as wholly and as perfectly as if that one were the only one, what hinders us from receiving the Mystery that He can cause His Living and Life-giving Body to be present for the participation of every Believer, whensoever the conditions that He requires are fulfilled?

What we want, then, in coming to this most Holy Communion, is, not of any necessity, *hot feelings*, but rather *a firm faith* in our LORD's Words here spoken to us. For our LORD's Presence here does not depend on our feelings, but on His own Promise. That Promise does not change as our feelings do. To think that we have not CHRIST unless our feelings are greatly moved and excited, argues a great want of faith in the unchangeable Promises of GOD. [See Note B.]

TRANSUBSTANTIATION.

They who hold this peculiar Doctrine believe that *the whole Substance of the Bread is changed into the Substance of the Body of Christ;* and similarly of the Wine.

We can believe easily enough that this is possible with GOD, for it does not seem a greater Miracle of His Power than many others which we believe, such as, for instance, *the changing of Water into Wine*, at our LORD's very first Miracle.

So that if this doctrine be clearly revealed to us, or

if it follow of necessity from one that is clearly revealed, we should find no difficulty whatever in believing it.

Only, we cannot believe that GOD requires us to disbelieve the evidence of our own senses. So that they who hold this doctrine of Transubstantiation hold that although the earthly Substance of the Bread is gone and changed into the spiritual Substance of our LORD's Body; yet the *qualities* or *properties* of the natural substance of Bread all remain; its colour remains, its hardness or smoothness remains, its taste remains, its look remains, its smell remains.

So that there is indeed here a miraculous exercise of the Divine Power in *two* respects; *first*, by Divine Power the *substance* of the Bread is removed, or annihilated, or changed; and *secondly*, all the natural properties or qualities of Bread are still supported, by a miraculous Divine Power, without the presence of the natural substance of which alone they are properties and qualities.

All this however we can believe to be possible with GOD, if He pleases so to exercise His Omnipotent Power.

But we may humbly consider, whether it is so revealed, or whether it follows as a necessary inference from what is revealed.

Now no one surely can say that this peculiar mode or manner of supernatural *change of substance* is distinctly revealed to us. Not a word is said about it.

But some affirm that it follows of necessity from our LORD's Words, " *This is My Body.*" Because it is argued, *A thing cannot be two things at one and the same time.* But, in this argument, the first word, "*A thing,*" must be defined. And we must consider that we are not simply speaking here of a mere ordinary Thing, but we are treating of a most profound and Heavenly Mystery.

And it does not in the least degree follow, as a

necessary inference, that the Presence of a Spiritual Substance with or in or under an earthly Substance should in any way whatever change or even in the slightest degree affect that earthly substance. The earthly substance does not of course absolutely fill the whole space that it occupies so as to exclude of necessity the Presence of a Spiritual Substance in that same space. The LORD's Spiritual Body passed through that closed door, and the earthly substance of the door remained perfectly unaffected. Why should the Presence of the LORD's Spiritual Body in or with or beneath the vail of the consecrated Bread affect or change the earthly substance of that element? The Heavenly Presence surely need not, of necessity, displace or change or even affect in any way the earthly presence.

Since therefore it is not revealed, and since it cannot be shown to be a *necessary* inference that the Presence of the Spiritual Substance of the LORD's Body changes or affects in any way the earthly substance of the Bread, we have no sufficient warrant to believe the doctrine of Transubstantiation. We dare not make it an Article of necessary Faith. An individual may perhaps without rebuke hold it as a private opinion, or as a pious belief, but it cannot be anything more. For it is, in reality, to affirm something, beyond revelation, as to the mode or manner of the Divine Presence in the Holy Eucharist. It is to make a statement *concerning Substances*, the laws and powers whereof are as yet altogether beyond our human knowledge.

We should much rather rest contented with believing both our bodily senses and our LORD's Words. Our bodily senses certainly assure us that *This is Bread*. But our faith in our LORD's absolutely precise and perfect words assures us also just as certainly that *This is His Body*. It would be doing violence to our senses not to believe it to be Bread in its natural substance; but it would be doing still more violence to our faith, not to believe it to be the Body of CHRIST.

We must therefore believe both what we see and what we hear. There is no contradiction; because the existence of what we see lies in the kingdom of Nature, and follows the laws of Nature: but the existence of what we hear lies in the kingdom of Grace, and follows the laws of Spirit and of Life with which we are unacquainted.

S. JOHN VI. 48—59.

It is impossible to have a proper understanding of the doctrine of the Holy Eucharist without a due consideration of our LORD's Discourse in the Synagogue at Capernaum related to us in the sixth chapter of S. John.

Some indeed have denied that this Discourse has any reference to the Holy Eucharist, because it was delivered before the Institution of the Eucharist. But it might be just as well denied that our LORD's Discourse with Nicodemus has any reference to Holy Baptism, because that Sacrament had not been then instituted. The truth rather is that we might have almost supposed of our own selves that our LORD would give instruction concerning both the Holy Sacraments before their actual Institution. Strange indeed it would have been, if our LORD had instituted the Holy Eucharist and given the Holy Communion of His Body and Blood to His Disciples, without ever having prepared them for it beforehand by discoursing to them concerning its nature.

Many things were said by our LORD to His Disciples, which they did not understand at the time, but which subsequent events enabled them to understand.

"*These things understood not His Disciples at the first; but when Jesus was glorified, then understood they that these things were written of Him.*"

No one can now read the Discourse in this sixth

chapter of S. John concerning the Holy Communion of the Body and Blood of CHRIST, and then go on to read the Account of the Institution of the Holy Eucharist without being almost of necessity convinced that the Discourse was preparatory to the Institution of the Sacrament, and intended to explain its nature and benefits.

Only let us put ourselves into the place of those first Disciples. They hear our LORD speaking of a marvellous truth of which they never heard before. He tells them that Except they eat the Flesh of the Son of Man and drink His Blood, they would have no Life in them: that this reception of His Body and Blood would give them Eternal Life, being the true Food and Sustenance of that Life; and that it would be the means of their dwelling in Him, and of His dwelling in them.

They did not understand the Mystery; some, taking our LORD's words only in a gross and carnal sense, were so much offended, that they went back and walked no more with Him.

But they whose faith endured the trial, who still followed the LORD, soon came to the night of the last Passover, and then they witness the Institution of a New Rite, a Rite which should take the place of that ancient Passover and be the distinguishing Rite of the New Dispensation: and, behold, the same LORD then speaks the amazing words, "*Take, eat; This is My Body. Drink ye all of this; This is My Blood.*"

Now those Disciples could not but think of our LORD's former words on this same great Mystery. The Discourse at Capernaum concerning the reception of His Body and Blood must surely have come into their minds. They could not but connect that Discourse with this Institution.

In the Discourse our LORD had said, "*Except ye eat My Flesh and drink My Blood, ye have no Life in you;*" now He says, "*Take, eat; this is My Body: Drink ye all of this; This is My Blood.*" Then He said that

He would give them certain Gifts necessary for their eternal Life, *now* He actually gives these Gifts to them.

For our gracious LORD would never surely reveal to us that certain Gifts are necessary for our eternal Life, without at the same time making provision that we should perfectly know how and when and where we are to receive Them.

The Institution of the Holy Eucharist, then, explains and completes the Revelation made in the Discourse at Capernaum.

In the Discourse we are very distinctly and most solemnly told that the Holy Communion of the Body and Blood of CHRIST is one thing necessary for our very eternal Life. In the Holy Eucharist the means of our receiving this most Holy Communion is most expressly ordained for us.

But we must now take notice of another Objection, one which is commonly made in our day.

Many say, that our LORD's words concerning "*eating His Flesh and drinking His Blood*" are merely figurative words, meaning only that which would be more commonly expressed by *receiving His doctrines, and profiting by His Death*. They understand the saying, "*Except ye eat the Flesh of the Son of Man and drink His Blood*," as being equivalent to this, "*Except ye believe in Me and trust in My Sacrifice.*" So that in this way there is no necessary connection between the Discourse at Capernaum and the Holy Eucharist; we may eat the Body and drink the Blood of CHRIST, at any time, and in any place, whenever we exercise faith in Him; in the Holy Eucharist indeed, but just as well anywhere else.

Now the Jews who heard the Discourse certainly did not understand our LORD's words in this sense. For if they had done so, there would have been nothing to offend them so very greatly. They need not have asked that question, "*How can this Man give us His Flesh to eat?*" If our LORD's words were merely an

Eastern metaphor, only meaning, "*Unless you have faith in Me, and receive My doctrines, you can have no Life in you,*" why were those Jews so offended at the language?

Besides, if those words only meant to express the familiar truth that our LORD would instruct them by His doctrine, and that they must believe it, if they would have Life, why did not our gracious LORD, in merciful condescension to their weakness, change His language, and lay aside the metaphor, and say that He only meant, what He had so many times said, "*Whosoever believeth in Me shall not perish, but shall have everlasting life?*" Instead of this, however, our LORD, when they were offended at His saying, repeated His startling statement, using again the very same words, even more strongly than before. So that no one can fail to perceive that our LORD first of all speaks of the spiritual necessity of *believing in Him* if we would have Life, and then proceeds to speak *of some distinct Gift* which He would give to those who should so believe in Him, namely, *His Body and Blood*. A plain distinction is made between *believing* Him or His doctrine, and thereupon *receiving* the True Meat and Drink which He would give for the sustenance of their Life in Him. We ought not to confound these two things together; they are as distinct as *believing in* the skill of a physician, and *taking* the medicine he orders.

Moreover, there is an end of all certain use of language, if we may suppose that our LORD only meant, "*Believe in Me,*" or "*Have faith in My Sacrifice,*" when, in the Institution of a positive Ordinance, He used the most extraordinary words, "*Take, eat; this is My Body.*" Surely our LORD'S words at such a moment would be the most perfect words and the most absolutely exact ones that human language could afford Him. And if in the Holy Sacrament we cannot think that the words, "*This is My Body,*" could be possibly changed into any others which would express our LORD's meaning in a better way, so no more may we think that the corresponding words in His Discourse at Capernaum may be changed into any others whatever.

Rather they reveal to us most distinctly one of the great Truths, one of the heavenly Mysteries of the Christian Religion. When St. Paul writes, "*The Bread which we break is the Communion of the Body of Christ*," he connects the Discourse and the Institution indissolubly together.

It is indeed a matter of the utmost surprise that any one should ever have doubted whether in His Discourse at Capernaum our LORD referred to the Holy Eucharist which He was about to institute. It is one of those instances in which so many moderns have drifted away so far from the judgment of the Primitive Church, and from what is really the most obvious and natural interpretation of Holy Scripture.

Here let us mark, by the way, that the three other Evangelists record the actual Institution of the Holy Eucharist, but S. John does not; he records the Discourse concerning its nature, just as he records the Discourse concerning the nature of the other great Sacrament but not its Institution. For this Evangelist, writing after the others, had for his special purpose to record those Discourses of our LORD which revealed most clearly the deeper Mysteries of the Christian Faith, the Trinity, the Incarnation, and the two great Sacraments.

From our LORD's Discourse, then, in this chapter of S. John's Gospel we learn these *five* several truths concerning the Mystery of the Holy Communion of His Body and Blood:—

First. That the Reception of these Divine Gifts is necessary for our Eternal Life. "*Except ye eat the Flesh of the Son of Man and drink His Blood, ye have no Life in you.*"

Secondly. We learn that these Divine Gifts constitute the true spiritual Food and Sustenance of our

Life in CHRIST. *"For My Flesh is Meat indeed, and My Blood is Drink indeed."*

Thirdly. That these Divine Gifts are the means by which the Power of an endless Life is now conveyed to us. *"Whoso eateth My Flesh and drinketh My Blood hath Eternal Life."* Not merely *shall have*, but *hath*, the power of Life now abiding in him.

Fourthly. That even our very bodies are preserved hereby unto the Resurrection in CHRIST. *"I will raise him up at the last day."*

And *fifthly.* To sum up all in one; for all our Eternal Salvation most essentially depends on our Union with our Divine Head, Who is our Life; we learn that the reception of these Divine Gifts is necessary for the preservation and continuation and strengthening of our Union with CHRIST. *"He that eateth My Flesh and drinketh My Blood dwelleth in Me and I in him."*

[See Note A.]

THE SIMILARITY OF THE MANNER OF OUR LORD'S TEACHING IN THE CASE OF BOTH THE SACRAMENTS.

It is to be remembered that S. John wrote his Gospel after the death of the other Evangelists, and that his object in writing it was not to repeat what had been written by the others, but much rather to fill up some particulars which they had omitted, and most especially to relate those Discourses of our LORD which set forth the deep Mysteries of His Kingdom, the Truths which belong distinctively to the Christian Revelation.

Accordingly we cannot but observe that S. John does not relate the history of the Institution of either of the two great Sacraments of CHRIST, for that had been sufficiently done by others before he wrote his Gospel. But he relates the Discourses of our LORD concerning the nature of these Sacraments; and it is very instructive to consider the great similarity in the manner of our LORD's teaching concerning them, thus related to us by S. John.

I. Our LORD perfectly foreknew all things, and in both cases alike He was pleased to give some instruction beforehand concerning the nature of those Sacraments which He meant to institute at their proper times. His Disciples did not well understand the things that were said to them at first, but our LORD sowed beforehand His words concerning His Sacraments as good and living seed in their hearts, that in due season they might spring up and bear fruit in His whole Church.

II. In both cases alike our LORD used the most solemn words possible: *"Verily, verily, I say unto thee, Except a man be born again, he cannot see the Kingdom of God."* *"Verily, verily, I say unto you, Except ye eat the Flesh of the Son of Man and drink His Blood, ye have no Life in you."* What words could be stronger? When therefore we consider Who He is Who spoke them, how greatly should our whole soul be arrested; how earnestly and reverently should we ponder in our hearts these Sayings of the SON of GOD. Heaven and earth shall pass away, but His Words cannot.

Surely, then, our LORD must here intend to declare to us some exceedingly great Truths; surely here there must be some new Revelations, not made known unto the Saints of old; surely here there must be some Mysteries of CHRIST most necessary for all His Disciples to know and to hold.

III. The absolute statements are in both cases alike so very exclusive; No one can enter into the Kingdom, except he be born of Water and of the Spirit: and, No one can have Life abiding in him, except he receive the Body and Blood of CHRIST.

IV. In both cases alike, the hearers were startled and perplexed greatly. They made answer to the LORD, as if they were perfectly at a loss, and quite unable to believe. One said, "*How can a man be born when he is old?*" And the others said, "*How can this Man give us His Flesh to eat?*"

V. Now if our LORD had used words, as we sometimes do, in a hurry, so that they might be qualified or changed into others, or if He had used merely a figure of speech, so that He might lay it aside; if the Mysteries involved in our LORD's startling words could have been declared in other human words with equal propriety, so that they might be words more easy of reception on the part of those as yet weak in faith; doubtless we may humbly think that our LORD would have so modified or changed them, in His great tenderness and compassion towards the weak. For He Who teaches us that we ought not to offend a weak brother, would not Himself have offended any by any startling words, if those words were not necessary. But instead of doing this, we mark, our LORD in both cases alike repeats His words, even in the second case using still stronger ones. One mistake indeed He did at once remove, telling His hearers that He was not speaking of mere natural flesh and blood, as they supposed, for *that* would certainly profit nothing; He took away their gross conception, but He left His Sayings all untouched in their true sense, as relating to the powers of the Spirit and of Life. For He spoke of His spiritual Body, not of His natural.

VI. The word "*except*," then, remains in all its force in both cases alike, teaching us with the most Divine authority the essential necessity of both the great Sacraments of the Gospel; for this similarity in both cases could not surely have been without knowledge and intention on our LORD's part. Our attention therefore is most forcibly called to these holy Mysteries of CHRIST, as pertaining to the very Life of our souls.

VII. Next let us consider that in both cases alike our LORD directs His hearers to the Ascension. As much as to say, *Wait till the Son of Man ascends into* the glory of the Father, then you will understand these Mysteries in a better way. For from My Ascension it is that they derive all their power.

For He ascended in order "*that He might fill all things,*" in order that the Church might be constituted in Him, and be "*the Fulness of Him Who now filleth all in all.*" (Eph. iv. 10, and i. 23.)

So the occasion of the Institution of Holy Baptism was made to be the very Ascension itself; thus teaching us that on the Ascension of our Incarnate LORD, the true Ladder was set up between Heaven and earth, and by our Baptism we are joined on to Him our Divine Head reigning in glory. And it is also of His ascended glorified Body that He speaks in the Holy Eucharist, by participation in Which our Union with our Life-giving Head is preserved.

VIII. Lastly, our LORD seems to have been grieved when they who were offended left Him, for He said to the Apostles, "*Will ye also go away?*" But yet He would not withdraw His Sayings in order to conciliate the objectors and bring them back. Our LORD would not modify one word, for not one word had been uttered at random; every word was perfect and necessary for the due declaration of the truth to the whole Church.

So that we plainly learn that there is a deep Mystery in the Sacraments of CHRIST, such as the natural man cannot receive, such as the unbelievers will ever scoff at. But, for all that, the Church must hold and declare the Mystery at all risks. The doctrine of the Sacraments has been from the first, and ever will be to the end, an occasion of offence; many will draw back. But the Church must be faithful, and not abate one word of her teaching concerning them, nor concerning their great necessity in order to Salvation in CHRIST. Their supernatural greatness must be plainly and strongly set forth, whether men believe, or whether they draw back.

S. PAUL'S COMMENTARIES.

"*As often as ye eat this Bread and drink this Cup, ye do show the Lord's Death.*" (1 Cor. xi. 26.)
"*The Cup of blessing which we bless, is it not the Communion of the Blood of Christ? The Bread which we break, is it not the Communion of the Body of Christ?*" (1 Cor. x. 16.)

S. Paul was not present himself at the Institution of the Holy Eucharist, but, as he tells us, (1 Cor. xi. 23,) he received the knowledge of this holy Mystery by direct revelation from the LORD. This very circumstance, however, seems to add great confirmation to our faith concerning the unspeakable importance of this Holy Mystery of CHRIST; and every word spoken by the Apostle, who was thus taught by direct revelation, on this great truth, ought to receive from us the most reverent attention, as if indeed spoken by the LORD Himself. Next to the Words of Institution themselves, these words of S. Paul should be considered; for here is an inspired Commentary on our LORD'S own Words.

The first great truth that appears at once, when we read these words of S. Paul, is this: that in the doctrine of the Holy Eucharist there are certainly two leading ideas: one, that as often as we celebrate it, *we show the Lord's death;* the other, that it is also *the Holy Communion of the Body and of the Blood of Christ*.

We must not, therefore, on any account fail to believe these two great truths concerning the nature of this Divine Institution.

Whenever we celebrate the LORD'S Supper, *we show the Lord's Death*, we show the One only true Sacrifice, the Sacrifice of the Death of the Incarnate SON of GOD; the full, perfect, and sufficient Sacrifice, Oblation, and Satisfaction for the sins of the whole world. We show this Sacrifice, before the world, before ourselves assembled together, and before the FATHER. Of necessity, the chief thing to be considered is, that we show the LORD's Death, *before the eyes of God the Father*. We assemble ourselves together for Divine Worship, and this is the chief Act of our Worship; we show forth, we represent in the peculiar manner appointed for us by our LORD Himself, we plead, we offer before GOD, our one only plea for mercy and life; we come before GOD, in our chief Act of worship *showing the Sacrifice of His Son*. There is no other Act of Christian Worship like this.

Then, the other part of this Holy Institution follows: the Bread which we herein break is the Communion of the Body of CHRIST, and the Cup of blessing which we herein bless is the Communion of the Blood of CHRIST.

These words are very express. The word *Communion* in the original language strictly means, *participation of*, or *communication of*, or *being made one with*. So that we are here infallibly taught that the broken Bread and the blessed or consecrated Cup are means or vehicles, or instruments, by which we are made partakers of the Body and of the Blood of CHRIST. It would evidently be altogether below the meaning of these words, to believe that the consecrated Elements are merely signs or figures of the absent Body and Blood of CHRIST. Rather, the Apostle certainly declares that by receiving these consecrated Elements we receive, verily and indeed, the Body and the Blood of CHRIST. Here is the actual partaking of these Heavenly Gifts. This is the Means, Divinely appointed, whereby we receive, in a most heavenly and supernatural Mystery, the Body and Blood of Him Who is our Life.

Here is the very greatness of the Sacrament. It consists of two parts: one is the outward visible sign, which is only humble and lowly, only the ordinary and natural substances of Bread and Wine; but the other part is the inward spiritual Grace, invisible and supernatural, even the spiritual Substance of the Body and Blood of CHRIST. By receiving the outward part we receive also the inward. The Bread, broken and consecrated in this Holy Mystery, is the present and actual Communion or Participation of the Body of CHRIST.

We learn then from S. Paul's commentaries that this Holy Institution of CHRIST has a double purpose: it is for our chief Act of Christian Worship, as the showing of the Sacrifice of the LORD's death; and it is, at the same time, our true Feast upon that Sacrifice, it is the Holy Communion of the Body and Blood of CHRIST.

Both these parts of the most essential nature of the Holy Eucharist must ever be kept in view.

And it is easy to see how exactly these two doctrines are contained in the words used by our LORD Himself at the Institution; one of them in the words, "*This do, in remembrance of Me;*" and the other in, "*Take, eat'; This is My Body;*" "*Drink ye all of this, for This is My Blood.*"

THE BENEFIT.

"*What profit is it, that we have kept His Ordinance?*" (Mal. iii. 14.)

The Benefit of observing any Divine Institution must of necessity be real and great. In keeping any of the Commandments of GOD there must be a great reward. If GOD orders anything for us, it must be *intended* for our benefit; and if we do what He bids, He will surely give us the Benefit intended.

We ought indeed to obey the command of GOD, simply because He commands us, and not for the sake merely of obtaining the benefit intended. But yet it is not wrong to desire the benefit intended. Rather it would be wrong *not to desire* what GOD promises. And when any particular Benefit is promised and described, it becomes us to consider its nature with care.

It does not follow, however, that we must be able in all cases immediately to perceive the benefit. Indeed the benefit and reward of keeping the Commandments of GOD will never be *fully* perceived by any of us, till the Resurrection Day; *then* it is that our LORD has said that He will bring His Reward with Him.

Nor does it follow that we must be able, in all cases, to understand at the time what the Benefit is. As it often is, in the case of some grievous affliction; the benefit is "*afterward*," (Heb. xii. 11,) and is not at all understood or realized *at the time ;* even so it may be, in other cases also. Or, the Benefit may be altogether beyond the perception of our bodily senses, and altogether above our human reason. It may belong only to the powers and glories of the world to come; it may relate only to the Laws of Spirit and of Life, which are at present very far beyond the reach of our knowledge.

Nor again, must we, on any account, judge of the true and real Benefit which there may be in keeping any Divine Law or Institution, by any present feeling. There is indeed a very grievous fault and a very dangerous mistake prevailing on this point amongst many people. They think that when their feelings are much moved, they no doubt receive much good to their souls. If they hear the good Word of GOD with many feelings of joy and pleasure, they take it for granted at once, that they get much benefit. They measure the good that they get, at any religious Service, by the degree in which their feelings are moved. They believe that if they experience hot feelings, it is a sure sign that the LORD is with them and blessing them.

Now although our feelings *ought* to be very deeply moved at the infinitely great truths of the Gospel, yet it is quite possible, and quite common, that these deeply-moved feelings should soon cool down and wear off and bear no good fruit. As our LORD Himself so plainly describes it: "*These are they, which, when they hear, receive the Word with joy; and these have no root, which for a while believe, and in time of temptation fall away.*"

So that it is very dangerous to think that mere transitory feelings, however good and right they may be, are in themselves any test of the reality of our religion, or any proof of getting real good to our souls. If we judge of the Benefit that we receive, merely by our feelings at the time, we are in exceeding great danger of deceiving our own selves in the matter of religion. Very often it may happen that we receive *most* real benefit, when our feelings are not at all moved or excited.

Let us, then, bearing these things in mind, consider, so far as is permitted us, what is *the special Benefit* intended for us in the Holy Institution of the Eucharist.

This we must learn from the very nature of the Institution itself.

As this nature is twofold, so is also the Benefit of it twofold.

The essential Nature of the Holy Eucharist consists in its being the only Divinely-ordained Means for showing the Sacrifice of the Death of CHRIST, and in its being the only Divinely-ordained Means of our receiving the Body and the Blood of CHRIST.

And accordingly the Benefit intended for us depends upon these two truths.

PART I.

If our LORD Himself has instituted and ordained for us one very peculiar and special Means for showing, before the FATHER, in our chief Act of Worship, the Atoning Sacrifice of His Death, then it follows of necessity that, as often as we "*do this*" in true repentance and faith, we are made partakers of the benefit of that all-atoning Sacrifice, in such a special manner as we are not at any other time. We are made partakers of the Atonement. This indeed is most distinctly taught us by the Words of our LORD Himself, Who, as He holds out to us the Cup which He consecrates in the Eucharist, says to us individually, "*This Cup is the New Covenant in My Blood.*" Here, therefore, the LORD Himself places in our own hands the very Sign and Seal of the New Covenant which is established with us by the Sacrifice of His Death. This is certainly nothing less than saying that here we are made *partakers of the Atonement*. "*This is My Blood* (our LORD says) *of the New Covenant, which is shed for the remission of sins.*" And This He Himself communicates to us in this Holy Sacrament. We cannot, therefore, fail to understand that this is the one Divinely-appointed Means for applying to us individually the Benefit of the All-atoning Blood-shedding of the SON of GOD.

At *all* times, indeed, we must trust in this Sacrifice, we must depend upon it, we must hope in it, we must mention it before the FATHER as our one only ground of prayer.

But here, in this Holy Eucharist, is a Means instituted by CHRIST Himself, in and by which, if truly penitent, we are actually made partakers in that Sacrifice; the all-atoning Blood is applied to us individually; *we receive the Atonement*.

For it is *one* thing, we should consider, that *there should be* an all-sufficient Sacrifice for sins; but it is *another* thing that there should be a Means instituted by the LORD Himself by which the Benefit of that Sacrifice is *applied to us* individually; just as it is *one* thing that there should be Life in CHRIST, but *another* thing that we should be made partakers of it.

It is as much beyond our own power to apply the Sacrifice of CHRIST to our own selves, as it is to make ourselves live. The *application* of the Sacrifice to individuals is as much the work of GOD as the very *making* of the Sacrifice.

This, therefore, is one most unspeakably great and precious Benefit of the Holy Eucharist; in it we are made *partakers of the Atonement;* it is an Application of the Benefit of the One Sacrifice to our own selves.

PART II.

The other essential part of the Nature of the Holy Eucharist is, that it is the Divinely-ordained Means for our receiving the Heavenly Gifts of the most precious Body and Blood of CHRIST. It is the Holy Communion.

Now in our LORD's Discourse in the synagogue at Capernaum, recorded in S. John vi., the Benefit of this Holy Communion is most expressly revealed to us.

Let us, then, consider this portion of Divine Revelation with all care and reverence.

First, our LORD says, "*Except ye eat the Flesh of the Son of Man, and drink His Blood, ye have no Life in you.*" We may have ever so many pious wishes and good feelings, but yet "*no Life,*" that is to say, *no eternal Life abiding in us.* Our very eternal Life, our LORD most solemnly assures us, depends, amongst other things, upon our receiving His most precious Body and Blood. In the Order of what is necessary for our great Salvation, these Divine Gifts are certainly necessary.

The essential Benefit here intended for us, we see, therefore, at once, belongs to the very Power of eternal Life.

For again our SAVIOUR speaks on this point, and says, "*As the Living Father hath sent Me, and I live by the Father; so, he that eateth Me, even he shall live by Me.*" As the Life of the SON is by the FATHER, even so our Life is by the Incarnate SON. Our Life is in Him; He is our Life; and it is necessary to the preservation of this our Life in CHRIST, that we receive His most precious Body and Blood; "*He that eateth Me, even he shall live by Me.*" "*For My Flesh is Meat indeed, and My Blood is drink indeed.*"

Here therefore, we learn, here is the very Food and Sustenance of our Life in CHRIST. As our Communion Office expresses it:

"*Almighty God, our Heavenly Father, hath given His Son our Saviour Jesus Christ, not only to die for us, but also to be our spiritual Food and Sustenance in this Holy Sacrament.*"

Here let us consider that GOD alone is self-existing. He alone is the one eternal *I AM*, requiring no support out of Himself. But for the Life of every created being, *some* support and sustenance, according to its nature, is necessary; namely, whatever GOD has made and appointed to be so. Even so it is with respect to our souls. They are spiritual substances, not self-existing, not having eternal Life in themselves, but deriving it from GOD, and requiring such spiritual Food and Sustenance as GOD has made necessary. And this Food and Sustenance of our New Life in CHRIST consists, our LORD here teaches us, in His most precious Body and Blood. Of course this is a great Mystery, belonging to the Laws of eternal Life, relating to the Power of the Spirit, not to the flesh and blood of this mortal life. "*My Words are Spirit,*" says our LORD, "*and they are Life.*" We must not interpret them by the laws of nature; we must not judge them by any present senses or feelings that we may possess: they are Divine, supernatural Words, belonging to the Eternal and Divine Powers of Life and Spirit; and therefore they are more true and real than any words which belong merely to the laws of time and of sense. The Benefit of this Holy Communion pertains to the very Life of our souls; it cannot be judged of in the least degree by any present feelings; we must judge of its unspeakable greatness, simply, by faith in our SAVIOUR's own words respecting it. By them let us be guided, rather than by any mere weak transitory feelings.

For again our LORD speaks and says, "*Whoso eateth My Flesh, and drinketh My Blood, hath Eternal Life; and I will raise him up at the last day.*" Even *now*, a faithful partaker of the Body and Blood of CHRIST "*hath Eternal Life;*" not only he *shall* have it, but he "*hath*" it already, as a Seed sown in him, which shall expand at last into fruits of heavenly Glory. And this Seed of Eternal Life, this quickening Power, is planted within our *whole* being; for "*I will raise him up, at the last Day.*" The Resurrection of our very *body* unto eternal life depends, we thus learn, on this most Holy Communion. By this heavenly Communication of the spiritual Substance of the very Body and Blood of CHRIST, our own whole being is quickened with Eternal Life. These Divine Gifts are the very Food of Immortality, both for our body and for our soul.

But here let us observe what takes place with regard to our natural food; for the likenesses between the Works of GOD in Nature and His higher Works in Grace are very remarkable and manifold and instructive. Our common food operates, for the support and sustenance of our bodily life, only very insensibly and by slow degrees. We do not usually judge of its real benefit merely by the feelings of the moment. Bad unwholesome food might stimulate us for the moment, so that we might feel at the time very strong and well, and yet, after awhile, our bodily life might be injured and lessened by it; whilst, on the other hand, the food that is really best for us may *seem* at the time not so pleasant, and even to do us no good. But by eating and drinking proper food every day, we find that our bodily life is preserved in proper vigour. And yet we do not ourselves know *how* this effect is produced. So it is with respect to our Eternal Life. The particular manner in which the Divine Food given us in the Sacrament operates within the very substance of our being, we know not. It is enough that we hear and believe our SAVIOUR's Words; and that, depending upon their absolute truth, we seek continually for this Bread of Life, in the way that He has ordained. So shall we obtain the real strengthening of our souls, the real preservation of our eternal Life; although, it may be, by insensible degrees.

But, once more, let us listen to the other sentence of our SAVIOUR's teaching concerning the unspeakable Benefit of this most Holy Communion: "*He that eateth My Flesh and drinketh My Blood, dwelleth in Me, and I in him.*" Now no gift of the Grace, and of the Power, and of the Love of GOD, can be greater, none higher, none more glorious, none more essential to our Eternal Life, than this Gift of Union with Him Who Alone is our Life. "*God has given to us Eternal Life; and this Life is in His Son.*" This our Eternal Life is derived to us from the SON of GOD Incarnate, Who is our New Life-giving Head. We have Eternal Life only through our union with our Divine Head. And this Union is preserved and continued to us, our LORD here teaches us, by our reception of His most precious Body and Blood. By these Divine Gifts we are made one with Him, and He one with us. Our mystical Union with Him Who is our Life-giving Head is hereby sustained and preserved. And on this Union all our great Salvation most nearly and essentially depends.

CONCLUSION.

Oh, how ill, then, must they be instructed, how little and weak must be their faith, who ask that question of impatience and of unbelief, "*What profit is it that we have kept His Ordinance?*" (Mal. iii. 14.) Surely all such must be judging by sight and sense, and not by faith.

Oh, how faint and feeble, and ready to perish, must be the Life of those who, like the Israelites in the wilderness, complain of the miraculous Food which GOD has provided for them, saying, "*Our soul loatheth this light Bread*," (Numb. xxi. 5,) whilst they desire food which is more stimulating and exciting to the natural feelings; which after all is only natural Food, not really spiritual and Divine; causing, perhaps, our mere natural mind to be more pleased and interested at the moment, but in reality injuring and starving the true Life of our souls, whilst we mistake the luxury of indulgence in warm feelings for the Life of faith.

Let us rather guide ourselves, in the humble patience of obedient faith, by the words of the LORD Himself.

These, if we duly consider and understand them, certainly teach us, that, in this His own most Holy Ordinance, we are made partakers, from time to time, of the Benefits both of the Atonement and of the Incarnation of the SON of GOD. This is the only Divinely-ordained Means whereby we are made partakers of the Sacrifice of the Death of our LORD, and also of the Power of that Life which is in Him as our Divine Head.

The Benefit, therefore, in both respects, whether we regard the Sacrifice or the Communion, is indeed next to infinite.

THE QUICKENING FLESH OF THE SECOND ADAM.

"*The Last Adam was made a Quickening Spirit.*" (1 Cor. xv. 45.)

We may well again consider, more distinctly, the great question, *What is the end or purpose, for which the Holy Communion of the Body and Blood of Christ is granted unto us?* For doubtless so heavenly and unspeakable a Gift cannot be given unto us, but for some exceedingly great and necessary purpose.

It might have been that this purpose should not

have been at all revealed unto us. If it had been so, still we should have obediently received the Holy Communion, steadfastly believing that it was a Divine Gift in some way above our present knowledge unspeakably beneficial to us and necessary for our Salvation.

But our SAVIOUR has been pleased to reveal unto us in some degree *the great purpose* for which it is necessary that we should be made partakers of His Body and Blood.

One thing we all know and believe very firmly, that our Life is in CHRIST our Divine Head; "*He is our Life;*" "*Our Life is hid with Christ in God.*"

For this very purpose has the Eternal SON of GOD become Incarnate, that He may be to us a Second Adam, a New Head, a Fresh Source of Life. He is our New Living and Life-giving Head.

For Life must not only be purchased *for us*, but as well communicated *to us*.

"*God hath given unto us Eternal Life, and this Life is in His Son. He that hath the Son hath Life; and he that hath not the Son, hath not Life.*" (1 S. John v. 11, 12.)

Our Eternal Life, then, we know, is derived to us from GOD the SON Incarnate. For "*As the Father hath Life in Himself, so hath He given to the Son to have Life in Himself;*" and the SON Incarnate now communicates of this Life to us His Members. By His Incarnation He is made *the True Vine;* He is the Life-giving stem, and we being grafted into that Stem and made Branches in Him, receive of the Sap of that Living Stem. Our Life is thus derived to us, through our union with CHRIST, the Incarnate SON of GOD, our Divine Head, the Second Adam. Not only has the Incarnate LORD given His Life *for us*, but He also now gives His Life *to us*.

Both these Gifts are equally required for our Eternal Salvation from sin and death. An external Sacrifice for sin alone would not save us, without also an internal Power of Life. CHRIST our SAVIOUR is therefore both our Sacrifice for sin, and as well our indwelling Life-giving Head; according to those words of the Apostle, "*know ye not, how that Jesus Christ is in you, except ye be reprobates?*" And so also we meet with the expression, "*Eternal Life abiding in him.*" (1 S. John iii. 15.)

Thus the Second Adam is made unto us *a Quickening Spirit.* By His indwelling Spiritual Presence, He communicates to us the Power of an endless Life. Our Eternal Life is now communicated to us through our union and membership with our New Divine Head, the Incarnate SON OF GOD, just as our natural Life comes to us from our First Head. We can no otherwise receive our bodily natural Life, than by derivation of it from the first Adam, through our actual union and membership with him; and so in like manner our Eternal Life comes to us now only by derivation from the Last Adam, through our actual union and membership with Him.

And it is revealed unto us that this our Life in CHRIST depends for its support and nourishment and preservation within us, upon the Holy Communion of the Body and Blood of CHRIST. This is the exceedingly great purpose, for which this most Holy Participation is granted us.

This is distinctly revealed unto us by our LORD Himself in the sixth chapter of S. John.

The Jews asked our LORD, what sign or work He showed that they might believe Him. They said that Moses showed their fathers a great Sign, when he gave them the Manna from Heaven, and they asked, what Sign would our LORD show?

Then our LORD began to speak of that which was typified and prefigured by the Manna of old.

"*Moses gave you not that bread from heaven;* (it did not really come down from Heaven itself:) *but My Father giveth you the True Bread from Heaven. For the Bread of God is He which cometh down from*

Heaven and giveth Life unto the world." Here it is plain that our LORD, referring to the Manna of old which sustained the life of the Israelites in their journey to Canaan, is evidently speaking, not of giving Himself as a Sacrifice *for us*, but rather of giving Himself *to us* for our Life.

For then our LORD declares, contrasting the Manna of old, (which was only a Type and a Figure of the True) with the Food that He would give, "*Your Fathers did eat Manna in the wilderness, and are dead. This is the Bread which cometh down from Heaven, that a man may eat thereof, and not die. I am the Living Bread which came down from Heaven; if any man eat of this Bread, he shall live for ever. And the Bread that I will give is My Flesh, which I will give for the Life of the world.*" Now this surely is a most distinct and express Revelation indeed; declaring unto us most plainly the great Mystery that *the Flesh of Christ it is which quickeneth us with Life Eternal.*

The Jews then present, taking our LORD's words in a mere carnal gross sense, as if they were spoken of natural flesh, said, "*How can this Man give us His Flesh to eat?*"

But our LORD then repeated His words, in the strongest way possible: "*Verily, verily, I say unto you—Except ye eat the Flesh of the Son of Man and drink His Blood, ye have no Life in you.*"

And He added these words also: "*As the Living Father hath sent Me, and I live by the Father; so he that eateth Me, even he shall live by Me.*"

Now we must mark that when our LORD uses the words, "*The Bread that I will give is My Flesh,*" He expressly speaks of His Humanity; He declares that it is by our participation in His Flesh, that is to say, in His Human Nature, that our Eternal Life is derived unto us. We learn from our LORD's peculiar Words, that it is His Manhood which is communicated to us; that restored and perfect Manhood which now exists in the Second Man, our Living Divine Head, is communicated unto us; even *now* communicated in germ and power; and hereafter at the Resurrection to be fully developed in us, both in our body and soul, unto the glories of an endless life.

We do not pretend for a moment to answer that question of unbelief, " *How can this Man give us His Flesh to eat?*" even in its true meaning.

Only we must be sure to understand that it is of His risen ascended glorified Flesh for ever united to His Godhead, filled with the Powers of Life and of the Spirit, of which our LORD speaks, not of mere natural Flesh, which, of course, would profit us nothing.

The Second Adam, our Life-giving Head, the Quickening Spirit, gives even *Himself* unto us, in this most Holy Communion of His Body and Blood; " *He that eateth Me,*" He says. None of us can think or know, as yet, what essential influence and benefit this Holy Partaking of CHRIST has upon the very Life of our whole being.

But we must most thankfully and steadfastly believe our LORD's own express Words, " *He that eateth My Flesh and drinketh My Blood hath Eternal Life.*" He *hath* Eternal Life. The Power or Principle, the Seed or Germ, of Eternal Life is already planted within him. This is no figurative or metaphorical language. It is no mere promise of something future. The gift is present, real, immediate, already given to those who worthily partake of CHRIST by this Holy Communion of His Quickening Flesh. The Life that knows no end is already begun in them.

The Second Man, GOD the SON Incarnate, is thus therefore "*A Quickening Spirit,*" and the Holy Communion of His Body and Blood is the Means by which His Spirit quickeneth our whole Being with the Power of an Eternal Life.

" *He that eateth of This Bread, shall live for ever. And the Bread that I will give is My Flesh.*"

" Doth any one doubt, but that even from the Flesh

of CHRIST, our very bodies do receive that Life which shall make them glorious at the latter day; and for which they are already accounted parts of His Blessed Body?" (Hooker, v.)

And S. Ignatius calls this Bread of the Eucharist, "*the Medicine of Immortality, the Antidote of death.*"

We cannot but believe, therefore, that by means of this Holy Communion, a power of Life, distinct from our mere natural life, is conveyed to us, from our Divine Head; the seed of immortality is nourished within us, the rudiment of that spiritual body which shall be given us at the Resurrection is strengthened in us; the Eternal Life of our whole being is preserved in CHRIST.

To use the words of Hooker again: "That which quickeneth us is the Spirit of the Second Adam, and His Flesh that wherewith He quickeneth."

THE APPLICATION OF THE ATONEMENT.

In the Divine Institutions of the Jewish Law, and even before that Law, even from the beginning, Sacrifices were offered before GOD as acts of Atonement for sin. They were strictly Sin-offerings or Sacrifices for sin. The effect sought for was the Remission of the guilt and punishment of sin. Those ancient Sacrifices were not merely and only typical of the One Divine Sacrifice which was promised; they were themselves in some true sense and in some real degree *propitiatory* Sacrifices, they obtained actually the blessing sought for, they procured, when rightly offered, forgiveness of sin; they made Atonement, and the offerer received remission of sin.

Thus Job offered sacrifices for his sons, in order to obtain pardon for them; and when the Divine displeasure was moved against the friends of Job, GOD commanded that they should offer for themselves a burnt-offering, to avert the punishment due to their folly.

And in the fourth chapter of Leviticus we read, in several verses, "*the Priest shall make atonement for them, and it shall be forgiven them.*"

Now no one ever objects against this, that it interfered with the Atoning Sacrifice of CHRIST; we never say that these Divinely-appointed means of obtaining the forgiveness of sin were any disparagement of the one perfect and all-sufficient and only true Satisfaction which the LORD Himself made for the sins of the whole world once for all upon the Cross. We easily understand that in all these cases, the atoning virtue of the appointed Sacrifice was derived solely from the Sacrifice of the Cross, and in no way interfered with its exclusive greatness and preciousness. In fact, all those ancient Sacrifices for sin were nothing more than so many means and channels, Divinely-appointed, for applying to the individual offerers of them the merits of the Atoning Blood of the Incarnate SON of GOD. They were, for the time then present, *propitiatory*, because they were *means of applying* to the individuals who offered them the merits of Him Who is the One only Propitiation for sin.

In the same sense, therefore, we can easily understand how the Holy Eucharist is now for us *propitiatory*. It is ordained, for the time now present, to be, among other purposes, the channel or means of applying to us individually the benefit of the Atonement made by CHRIST for the sins of the world. In the Holy Eucharist, it may be most truly said, that we both offer the Atonement before GOD, and that we ourselves also individually receive the Atonement. It is the means Divinely-appointed whereby we individually *receive* the benefit of *the Atonement*. It is the channel appointed by CHRIST Himself through which we are individually *made partakers* of that Remission of sins which was procured for us by the Sacrifice of the Cross. This surely in no way whatever disparages or interferes with the all-essential truth that the Sacrifice of the SON of GOD on the Cross is the one only meritorious source of all Propitiation and Atonement for sin. It would be a grievous fault to imagine that there could be any such interference.

Now to show that the Holy Eucharist is instituted for this very purpose, amongst other purposes, namely, that in it there may be to us individually *an application of the Atonement*, we may use several arguments.

Take the case of the ancient Sacrifices. By Divine Institution there was not only the Sacrifice, but there was also *the Feast upon the Sacrifice*. And certainly the meaning of this peculiar Rite was that the Offerer of the Sacrifice received the benefit of the Sacrifice; he partook of the Sacrifice; he feasted, as it were, in GOD's Presence and with GOD; he was a partaker of the Table of the LORD; by eating of the Altar, he was made "*a partaker of the Altar*," (1 Cor. x. 18,) and so he had fellowship with GOD: the atonement he offered was accepted; peace was granted him.

Now the realization of those ancient Feasts upon the Sacrifice most evidently consists in the Holy Communion of the Body and Blood of the very Lamb of GOD, which we receive in the Holy Eucharist. This is the very Antitype, this is the truth and the reality itself. This Holy Communion is now for us, in Heavenly truth and reality, *the Feast upon the Sacrifice*. Taught infallibly, therefore, by those pre-ordained Rites, we know that we have, by means of this Holy and Divine Communion, the benefits of the Sacrifice of CHRIST given unto us; we are made partakers of the true Altar; we have individually herein fellowship with GOD; we eat and drink at the Table of the LORD; it is verily and indeed the application of the Atonement.

In the LORD's own appointed way, we offer and present unto GOD the one all-atoning Sacrifice for sin; and in return from Him we receive, each individual penitent for himself, an application of that Sacrifice.

Further, also, when our LORD instituted the Holy Eucharist, the very words He used prove that He instituted it to be a channel for the Remission of sin. For He said of the Cup of Blessing which we bless or consecrate in this Holy Sacrament, "*This Cup is My Blood, of the New Covenant, which is shed for you, and for many, for the remission of sins.*"

We cannot, therefore, surely be partakers of that Cup without partaking of this infinite benefit; we receive, if truly penitent, an individual share in this Remission of sins. It is, by Divine Institution, an application of the Atonement. Our souls are washed in the most precious Blood of CHRIST. We receive Him Who is the Propitiation for our sins. He Who is our Great High Priest executes His Priestly Office for us, and takes away our sin. He applies to us individually the Merits of His own all-atoning Sacrifice.

How great and unspeakable ought the comfort of this to be to every true believer in CHRIST. Just as in ancient times, by Divine Institution, the Priest offered the Sacrifice for a sinner, and thereupon his sin was forgiven; even so now, the Great High Priest Himself, ever ministering at the Heavenly Altar within the vail, whenever by His Command we here below celebrate this Holy Eucharist, and in it show forth His death; He lifts the one Eternal Sacrifice before the Presence of the FATHER, and obtains for us thereby pardon and forgiveness, even the Remission of sins; He applies to us the benefit of His own Atonement.

Thus, for our unspeakable comfort, we know, not only that there is an Atonement, not only that there is a Priest before GOD, not only that there is a Propitiation for the sins of the whole world; but we know as well that the LORD has also appointed a particular channel whereby the benefit of that Propitiation is conveyed to each penitent sinner; He has Himself ordained the means by which He applies to us the all-atoning Sacrifice of Atonement.

For we should certainly consider that we are no more able of our own selves to apply to our own selves the benefit of the Atonement, than we are able of our own selves to make that Atonement itself. Both the Atonement itself and its individual application must be alike the work of GOD, not of man.

It is true, we may at any time and in any place, believe in the Atonement, we may put all our trust in the Atonement, we may glory and rejoice in the Atonement; but yet all this is not the same thing as having a special Means, Divinely appointed for our use, in which the application of the Atonement is granted to us with Divine authority.

To believe that there is an all-atoning Sacrifice is one thing, but to be made actual partakers of it is another; just as of old time, to offer the Sacrifice was *one* act, but to partake of the Feast upon the Sacrifice was *another* act. Both acts alike must be done upon Divine institution and authority, or else they are merely human inventions, self-made and unauthorized, unable to bring us near to GOD, leaving us still in doubt and suspense.

THE EUCHARISTIC SACRIFICE.

The importance of this part of the nature of the Holy Eucharist is so exceedingly great, that it must be here treated separately, although at the risk of repeating some truths which have already been considered.

It is a most fundamental article of our Christian faith that the Incarnate SON of GOD, by the one sacrifice of Himself on the Cross, made a full, perfect, and sufficient satisfaction for the sins of the whole world. No other sacrifice for sin is needed. If any man sin, his sin can be taken away by no other sacrifice, but only by the Sacrifice of the Death of CHRIST;

his soul can be washed clean from all sin only through the most precious Blood of the Lamb of GOD. There never was, and never can be, any real Atonement for sin, but only the Sacrifice of the Eternal SON of GOD.

In his Epistle to the Hebrews S. Paul takes great pains to show to the Jewish Believers in CHRIST the superiority of the Christian dispensation over the Jewish. He proves that the Jewish dispensation was only a temporary one, and that it was a type and pattern of the Christian. Throughout the Epistle S. Paul speaks of the many Jewish Sacrifices, and contrasts with them the one Christian Sacrifice, namely, that made by CHRIST. He says that the Jewish Sacrifices were continually repeated, that they were many and of various kinds, that they were all of themselves unavailing to take away sin, and that they were only shadows and types of the one Sacrifice which CHRIST Himself was to offer once for all.

Now the question here is, what is the proper meaning of the word "*once*" thus used by the Apostle? What is it that CHRIST Himself was to do *once for all?* Surely the Apostle means this: that as those Jewish Sacrifices were many, and continually repeated, each Sacrifice being a fresh Sacrifice, so, on the contrary, the Christian Sacrifice is but one, and is never repeated; that is, CHRIST Himself, the True Lamb of GOD, was to endure Death but once. He offered Himself to suffer death in sacrifice for our sins once, and once only. His most precious Blood was shed once only. He redeemed us once for all; He made Atonement by His actual Death once only. When He died, He finished all His suffering for sin. The Sacrifice of the Cross was never to be repeated. The value of that Sacrifice was infinite. This is the one only true Atoning Sacrifice; the one only Fountain, from which alone all virtue had been derived all along from the beginning for any atonement or propitiation for sin. "*The Blood of Jesus Christ,*" this and this alone, from first to last, "*cleanseth from all sin.*"

We could not believe anything which would in the slightest degree interfere with this most fundamental truth of the Christian Revelation. We could not believe anything which would in the remotest degree disparage this all-precious truth.

But now let us call to mind another and equally precious truth. What is our LORD doing *now*? what Office is He discharging for us continually *now*? It will be said at once that He is now our Great High Priest, and that He is now ever living, at the Right Hand of the FATHER, to make Intercession for us. Consider, then, what this Priestly Intercession means. It does not merely mean that our LORD is only praying for us, just as any righteous man might pray for us. To think that this is all, would be very much below the infinite mystery of our LORD's Intercession.

Our LORD's present and continual Intercession, in the true Sanctuary above, as the Priest of His Church, is as great and as necessary a part of His Work for our salvation, as His Death upon the Cross. "*Having been reconciled by His Death, much more shall we be saved by His Life,*" is the language of S. Paul. The Cross and Passion "*once for all*" may not, therefore, be separated in our thoughts from the present continual ever-living Intercession. Our LORD not only *was* our Priest when He offered Himself on the bloody Cross, but He is still our Priest in Heaven. He is continually executing for us the Office of a Priest before the FATHER.

Now the essential character of this our LORD's present Priesthood was very expressly foreshown and clearly typified by GOD's own Institutions in the Jewish Church. When the chief Act of Atonement once a year was to be made for the sins of the whole year, the High Priest was to enter in within the vail, and to appear in the presence of the Mercy-Seat of GOD; but *not without blood:* he was to carry in with him the blood of the Sacrifices which were slain in the outer court, and to offer and present those Sacrifices before the special Presence of GOD by means of the presentation of the Blood of those Sacrifices; covering the Mercy-Seat at the same time with the clouds of Incense, which was burnt with fire from off the Altar of burnt Sacrifice.

The Blood of the Sacrifice carried the whole Sacrifice; for the Blood is the Life. So that the offering of the Sacrifice was not completed until the Blood was thus brought in before GOD. The Action was all *one* Action, but it was not completed until the High Priest thus entered in within the vail.

All this Divinely foreordained type and figure is now perfectly fulfilled by the true Priest of the Church Himself in the Heavenly Sanctuary.

That which the typical Jewish Priest did *in the outer court*, in slaying and offering the animal on the Altar of burnt-offering, the LORD Himself, both Priest and Victim, fulfilled in infinite reality, once for all, in the outer court of this world; He laid down His Body on the Altar of the Cross, "*an Offering and a Sacrifice to God.*"

That also which the typical Jewish Priest did *within the vail*, in presenting the Sacrifice together with the Incense before the Mercy-Seat of GOD, the LORD Himself now also fulfils in infinite reality. He abides in the Presence of the FATHER for us a Priest for ever. He is performing *in reality* that which the Jewish Priest did *in figure*. He is presenting the One Sacrifice which He once made of Himself in Blood and Death on the Cross, and through this One Sacrifice He continually intercedes for us. He is offering within the vail in heavenly truth and infinite reality the Blood of the Sacrifice which was made once for all on the Cross. For as S. Paul writes, referring to this type, "*He entered in with His own Blood.*"

When S. Paul, therefore, speaks of *one* offering *once* made, he is contrasting the one actual death upon the Cross of CHRIST Himself with the many and repeated sacrifices made under the Jewish Law; but he is not speaking against the continual offering of this one sacrifice within the vail, on which depends the Intercession of our great High Priest before the FATHER.

The next point which calls for our consideration is this: Have *we* here on earth beneath simply and only *to think* upon our LORD'S past and present Work for our salvation; have we simply and only to *believe in it*, and to *trust in it:* or, is there any means, Divinely appointed for us, (for of course we could not devise or institute any such means of ourselves,) by which a present participation in the virtue and blessing and benefit of this Sacrifice and Intercession is actually now granted and assured to us? Is there any real link given to us, any connection established between our worship upon earth beneath and the Office of our great High Priest in Heaven above?

We certainly believe that all our worship below is accepted above, only through the Priestly Intercessions of our LORD. Is there any means, any Act of Worship, ordained for the Church below, which connects us with the Priesthood and Intercession of our great High Priest; or, is faith on our part the only thing required of us?

Here we are brought at once to the Holy Eucharist, which has been expressly ordained for His whole Church by the LORD Himself. This is no ordinary act of prayer or of praise. It is an Act of Worship instituted for us by direct Divine Authority; as much as the Sacrifices of old were instituted for Believers before.

Now *that* which the Holy Eucharist *was*, the *first* time it was celebrated, the *very same* it essentially *continues to be*, to the end of the world, every time it is celebrated.

Now at the *first* celebration of it, our LORD Himself was present; He appeared, for the first time, as a Priest according to the Order of Melchisedec; putting an end to the priesthood according to the Order of Aaron, He brought forth, not a bloody sacrifice of some slain animal, but the unbloody Oblation of

Bread and Wine; and having blessed these earthly creatures and made them to be the materials of His own distinctive Rite, He said of one, "*This is My Body, which is now given for you;*" and of the other, "*This is My Blood, which is now shed for you.*" Thus therefore the LORD Himself, both Priest and Victim, making good His own words, even then "*gave*" His Body and His Blood, in heavenly truth and profound reality, unto GOD, in sacrifice for us.

In that very first Holy Eucharist, the Sacrifice of the Cross was in a profound mystery offered and given unto GOD. The Body and the Blood of the very Lamb of GOD were therein, verily and indeed "*given*" unto GOD in sacrifice. It was not another Sacrifice, but the one only Sacrifice then "*given*" or offered.

And this one Sacrifice, then soon finished once for all in actual Blood and Death on the Cross, was carried in, on the Ascension, within the vail, and being so presented and offered before the FATHER became the ground of perpetual Intercession above.

This Holy Eucharist, then, being thus Divinely instituted and ordained for our continual use here below, as our one distinctive Christian Rite, and being still *to-day* the *very* same as at its *first* celebration, we plainly learn that we *have* a means Divinely ordained for us, whereby the Church on earth unites her worship with the ministrations of her Divine Head. Or, rather we should say, in this Holy Eucharist the LORD Himself is Himself ever present; He it is Who ministers here below, as well as there above; He it is Who really and alone blesses and consecrates the earthly elements; He it is Who ever makes good His own Words, "*This is My Body: this is My Blood;*" He it is Who acts as the true Priest by the hands of His earthly Ministers; He it is Who is still the Offerer of His own Sacrifice; ever uniting all in one; uniting the whole worship of the Church below, through His own Ministrations, with the worship at the heavenly Altar above.

By this Divinely-instituted means, therefore, we below are permitted to offer or present the one only Sacrifice before the Presence of the FATHER, in a profound and heavenly and tremendous Mystery.

There is not a shadow of interference with the one Sacrifice of the Cross; there is not the slightest thing done to disparage that one offering for sin. It is simply and only the offering of that one true and Divine Sacrifice which we continually offer and present, through union in this Holy Eucharist with the perpetual Ministrations of our Great High Priest, before the Presence of the FATHER.

The Sacrifice which we here offer is the Sacrifice of the Cross; only not in blood and death, but in an unbloody manner, namely, in that very same manner in which it was offered at the first celebration of this Divine Service.

And thus it is, and thus only, that the true Priest of the Church is ever discharging upon earth His Priesthood according to the Order of Melchisedec; for *He abideth a Priest for ever, after the Order of Melchizedec*, a distinctive part of which Order consists in this New Oblation of Bread and Wine, in the distinctive Rite of the Christian Dispensation.

The Sacrifice of the Cross is thus ever one and the same; it is the "*one Sacrifice for ever*," (Heb. x. 12;) it is one perpetual Sacrifice, never to be repeated, requiring no addition, full, perfect, and sufficient, applicable to every sin from first to last. It was *first* actually offered at the first Celebration of the Holy Eucharist, *then* made in blood and death on the Cross, and *now* perpetuated before the true Mercy-Seat above, and on the Altars of the Church below, through the continual Ministrations of our Great High Priest.

The Holy Eucharist is therefore not only *a Sacrament*, in which we receive the Body and the Blood of CHRIST for the Sustenance of our Life in Him unto eternal glory; but it is also *our Christian Sacrifice*, it is *the Eucharistic Sacrifice*, because in it this same Body and Blood of CHRIST are first of all "*given*" in sacrifice to GOD for our sins, just as they were at that first Institution.

This Holy Eucharist is thus the Means Divinely given us for presenting the One Divine Sacrifice before the Mercy-Seat of GOD, through a special act of our Great High Priest, Whose Intercessions reach down to us below in this His own Holy Service; for herein our worship on earth is united with the worship within the vail; and all essentially consists in the offering of the one Divine Sacrifice by the hands of the Great High Priest.

If the Holy Eucharist only contains *a figure* of the One Sacrifice, and is not the Means of our presenting that One Sacrifice itself, we should have for our chief Act of Worship nothing better than the ancient Jewish *figures of things absent*.

If the Holy Eucharist is not the Means whereby the One very Sacrifice of the Lamb of GOD is lifted up and presented before the true Mercy-Seat through the Ministration therein of our true Priest Himself, then there is no place left for the exercise of our LORD's Priesthood after the Order of Melchizedec, except we suppose that He presents the bare signs, mere Bread and Wine, *empty figures of something absent*.

It ought to confirm our faith in the doctrine of the Eucharistic Sacrifice most strongly indeed, when we consider how it has been held in the Church all along from the beginning. Let the reader only consider, for instance, the testimony of Irenæus. He wrote several books about one hundred and fifty years after the Crucifixion, which are universally received as his. When he was a young man, he says, he used often to see and hear the old Bishop of Smyrna, Polycarp, who was a friend of S. John's and had known several persons who had seen the LORD. He declares that he often heard from Polycarp an account of the Miracles and of the Doctrine of the LORD as he had received it from S. John. Surely, therefore, we may believe that Irenæus was more likely to know the mind of the Apostles on any great subject than people of the present day, who depend only upon their own ill-informed judgment.

Now Irenæus writes of the Holy Eucharist thus: "*Our Lord took that which is by creation Bread, and He gave thanks, saying, 'This is My Body;' and likewise the Cup, which is by creation that which it appears, He declared to be His Blood; thus delivering the New Oblation of the New Testament, which the Church, receiving it from the Apostles, offers to God throughout all the world.*"

Irenæus then proceeds to refer to the "*Pure Offering*" prophesied of by Malachi (i. 11,) "*My Name shall be great among the Gentiles, and in every place Incense shall be offered and a Pure Offering,*" that is, an Unbloody Offering. And having quoted this prophecy concerning the Gentile Church, he writes: "*The Prophet clearly signified by these words, that although God's ancient people should cease to offer sacrifice unto Him, yet that sacrifice should be offered unto Him in every place, and that an Unbloody Sacrifice;* [in distinction from the Jewish bloody Sacrifices:] *so that His Name should be glorified among the Gentiles.*"

Now this plainly testifies to the truth of the Christian Sacrifice in the Holy Eucharist. Irenæus declares that this great prophecy of Malachi concerning the times of the Messiah was understood in his day to refer to the Holy Eucharist, as being *the New Oblation* distinctively belonging to the New Christian Dispensation; and he says that "*the Church, receiving it from the Apostles, offered it throughout the world.*" And we cannot suppose that the Church throughout the world had at that time fallen into a mistake on so exceedingly great a matter; for Polycarp lived till within twenty years of this writing by Irenæus.

Let it be sufficient here to add extracts from two of our own Bishops.

Bishop Cosin writes: "*This is no new Sacrifice, but the same which was once offered, and which is every day offered to God by Christ in heaven, and continueth here still on earth by a mystical representation of it in the Eucharist.*"

Bishop Taylor writes: "*As Christ is a Priest in heaven for ever, and yet does not sacrifice Himself afresh, nor yet without a Sacrifice could He be a Priest, but by a daily ministration and intercession represents His Sacrifice to God, and offers Himself to God as sacrificed; so He does upon earth by the ministry of His servants. He is offered to God, that is, He is by prayers and the Sacrament represented or offered up to God as sacrificed.*"

THE SUITABLENESS OF THIS SERVICE TO OUR WANTS.

We may now perhaps understand in some better degree the great goodness of our LORD in providing for us such a Service as this is. Of course we could not but believe that if our LORD ordained any Service for His Church, it would be a Service *most exactly suitable* to our deepest feelings and to our most urgent wants.

Now what may we say are our deepest feelings and our most urgent wants, whenever we present ourselves before GOD for our chief Act of Worship?

Are they not feelings of our own most exceeding sinfulness in His all-holy eyesight? And are they not also feelings of our own helpless dying condition? Do we not most deeply feel that we are both *guilty* and *dying* creatures? Do we not feel that *pardon of sin* is not the *only* thing that we have need of, but as well *preservation of Life?*

And what may we say are the *two* chiefest things that our SAVIOUR came to procure for us? Are they not, *pardon of sin*, and *the gift of life?* For both these things are equally necessary to our eternal Salvation.

The Eternal SON of GOD was therefore made Man for these two great purposes; *one*, that He might give Himself *for us*, as an all-atoning Sacrifice for sin; the *other*, that He might give Himself *to us*, as an indwelling life-giving Head, a new source of immortal life, a second Adam, a quickening Spirit.

Our LORD has accordingly instituted this Holy Service for His whole Church, and in it He conveys to us individually, if we come to it in true repentance and faith, an actual and a present share in these inestimable benefits; benefits exactly suitable to our most urgent wants.

For in this holy and Divine Service we have the great means, appointed and given for our continual use, whereby we may present that One only atoning Sacrifice for sin, as our one only plea, in union with the Intercessions of our LORD Himself, before the FATHER, and whereby, at the same time, we may ever receive the Holy Communion of the LORD's Body and Blood for the continual sustenance of our eternal Life in Him.

Here therefore is the Divinely appointed means of conveying both pardon of sin to the guilty, and support of life to the dying.

In few words, therefore, in this our great Christian Service we are made partakers, from time to time, of the benefits both of the Atonement and of the Incarnation of the SON of GOD; than which nothing can be greater, nothing more glorious for us.

THE NECESSITY.

Although it must have been sufficiently plain, from many of the preceding considerations, that this Holy Sacrament is one of those things which it has pleased

GOD to make *necessary to our Salvation*, yet it may be well to state distinctly the *four* chief Reasons for teaching, as the Church does in her Catechism, that this Holy Communion is "*generally necessary to Salvation*," where the word "*generally*" strictly means "*to all men*," that is to say, of course, if the Sacrament can be had.

The *first* Reason arises from the very nature of the case. If our LORD Himself has been pleased to institute a certain Act of Worship for the use of His whole Church under this present Dispensation of His Grace, *how can it be supposed* that any Member of His Church who pleases may wilfully neglect it and yet be safe? If the Holy Eucharist be the one only Service Divinely appointed for us all by the Head of the Church, how may we venture to believe that we may trust in Him for Salvation, whilst we neglect the distinctive Service of His Religion?

The *second* Reason is founded on the nature of the Gifts which are offered us in this Sacrament. Can we indeed venture to think that Almighty GOD should offer us such infinitely great and precious Gifts as the Body and the Blood of His SON, if they were *not necessary* for the support of our Life in CHRIST? Surely we cannot think so. It is not for us to say, "*Why are these Gifts offered us?*" but seeing that they are offered us in this Holy Communion, who of us dare venture to say that they are *unnecessarily* offered us? Most surely it follows, that, if the Bread which we here break is the Communion of the Body of CHRIST, Who alone is our Life, it must be necessary to our Life in Him that we should partake of it.

The *third* Reason consists in the positive declaration of our LORD Himself on this very point. He would not leave us in any manner of doubtfulness on so vital a point. He has spoken on this point as solemnly as He has done on any point at all: "*Verily, verily, I say unto you, Except ye eat the Flesh of the Son of Man and drink His Blood, ye have no Life in you.*" And certainly our LORD has appointed and instituted no means of our receiving these His inestimable Gifts but only this Holy Sacrament. As plainly therefore as any one truth can follow from another, it follows that it is necessary to our Salvation that we come to this most Holy Communion of the Body and Blood of CHRIST our SAVIOUR. This is one of those things which GOD has made necessary in the order of our Salvation.

The *fourth* Reason confirms all that has been said, when we consider how manifestly the same Necessity was foreshadowed in all the ancient types and figures of this Sacrament. For these Types being themselves Divinely foreordained in all their essential particulars cannot mislead us on this point, all of them so remarkably agreeing thereupon.

In the case of the Tree of Life in the midst of Paradise, it was made *necessary,* if our first parents would sustain their immortal Life, that they should continually partake of the fruit of this Tree. It would have been the height of presumption in them if they had said, " *God is able to sustain our immortal Life without the fruit of this Tree.*"

In the case of the Passover, the Israelite who did not keep it when he was able, was to be cut off from the Congregation of the LORD, that is, he was to be excommunicated.

In the case of the Manna, there was no other Bread provided for the Israelites during their forty years' journey through the wilderness. It was their only sustenance till they reached the Promised Land.

And then in the case of all the Sacrifices all along from the beginning, what would have been the value of any Act of Worship, if the appointed Sacrifices were never offered by the Worshipper? If a Christian now offers Worship in the wilful neglect of the Holy Eucharist which is the only Act directly instituted and commanded by CHRIST, it must be the same kind of presumption as if an Israelite of old had offered worship in the wilful neglect of the Sacrifice then. Our Worship sinks into mere unauthorised self-invented worship, if it be disassociated from the Holy Eucharist.

Doubtless, therefore, we may conclude that it is the general Rule for all Members of the Church of CHRIST that it is necessary for them all that they come to this Holy Sacrament of CHRIST, if they desire to be saved by Him.

We have nothing to do with exceptional cases. We can believe that the very Heathen may be saved through CHRIST, although they know Him not, for their ignorance is not wilful. How many of them would believe in Him at once if we made Him known unto them! So also, perhaps, for some of us, we may humbly hope that as GOD is doubtless able, so He may be also willing, to save some who through pardonable ignorance, or through invincible prejudice do not receive this Sacrament of CHRIST. For GOD is doubtless able to convey the inward Grace of this Sacrament, without the outward part of it, when He pleases to do so, although He has not *said* or *revealed* anything on such exceptional cases. But we have *no right* to expect a Miracle, where the appointed Means of Grace are wilfully neglected. The Rule is plain and clear; all exceptional cases we must humbly leave in the Judgment of GOD, Who alone knoweth all things relating to each one.

THE FREQUENCY OF CELEBRATION.

At the time of Institution our LORD Himself said the words, "*As often as ye drink it.*" And S. Paul repeats the words, "*As often as.*" The Frequency, therefore, with which we are to "*Do this*" is not expressly ordered; it is left to our own decision.

But we should certainly mark the circumstance,

that our LORD *did* thus think of this very point. It was in His mind, that very moment, when He instituted this Holy Service; but He left it purposely to *our* decision. And surely He still regards it, He observes *how often* we do " *Do this ;*" surely He takes notice *how often* we do remember His last command.

Is there not, therefore, a trying of us, a proving of us, in this very matter of the Frequency of Celebration? Can we think of this, and not perceive that here is *some* test of our love?

In this matter, one person says, "*How often am I obliged to do this?*" And the Rule of the Church gives the positive but cold reply, "*Three times a year, at least;*" or else, you cut yourself off from the Church, your Church-membership is virtually at an end, you put yourself back into your heathen state.

In primitive times, if a member of the Church missed the Great Service for three Sundays together, he was excommunicated; but now, in these evil days, when the love of many has become so cold, to attend the Divine Service *three times a year* saves a man from excommunication.

But another person says, "*How often may I do this?*" And the answer to such is, "*There is no limit set to the frequency.*" "*As often*" as you have an opportunity given you, "*Do this,*" even *every day*, if you can.

But it may be well to consider, whether there is anything to direct us, in this matter, besides our own feelings.

Let us look back and see *how often* any Service of a similar nature was Divinely ordered to be offered to GOD in the Jewish Church. There we are forcibly struck at once by the Daily Sacrifice. Twice every day, at nine o'clock in the morning and at three o'clock in the evening, it was Divinely commanded that a Lamb should be offered to GOD in Sacrifice. (Exod. xxix. 39.)

Such was then the Frequency of the Public Service

at the Altar of GOD; even thus a Daily Sacrifice, "*a Continual Burnt Offering*," from generation to generation.

And what did the Sacrifice of that Lamb, every morning and every evening continually, foreshadow and signify? It was the Divinely-instituted means by which they then "*showed the Lord's Death.*"

And if that Daily Service and Worship had been omitted, would it not have been sin? Would it not have been evil, that GOD's peculiar and distinguishing Worship should be neglected? Does not the Prophet Daniel call it "*the abomination of desolation,*" that "*the Daily Sacrifice should be taken away?*" (xii. 11.)

May we not, therefore, conclude something from this for our own guidance, concerning the Frequency with which *we* should "*show the Lord's Death*" in our Divinely-instituted way?

Some Daily Service most certainly the Church of CHRIST ought to have; and what Service is complete without this one? If *they* had a Daily Sacrifice, why should not *we* have a Daily Eucharist? If the Showing of the Sacrifice of the very Lamb of GOD constituted *their* Daily Service, why should it not constitute *ours* also? If the distinctive Worship of the Jewish Dispensation was Divinely commanded to be offered *daily*, should the distinctive Worship of the Christian Church be offered less frequently? If the omission of the Daily Sacrifice was called by the Holy Prophet "*the abomination of desolation,*" *how much more* is the omission of the Holy Eucharist from week to week! To substitute other Services instead of this Divinely-appointed one does not remedy the "*desolation.*" To say the first half of the Service, as is so often now done, and then to leave off in the midst, has no other excuse, in the great majority of Churches, than mere custom, and that custom surely an evil one; for, as it has been not perhaps too severely said of it, it is the same kind of thing as if in our own houses we should say Grace over an empty table.

It must be allowed, indeed, that there is in our case no positive Law concerning this Frequency, as there was in the Jewish Church. But, is it necessary that there should be? Has the Disciple of the LORD JESUS as much need of a positive Law in this matter as the Disciple of Moses? Is not the very nature and reason of the thing quite enough to decide the matter, in the mind of every one who loves the LORD JESUS in sincerity?

But what was the practice of the Apostles, and of the Primitive Church, in this matter? For this most surely ought to guide us very greatly indeed.

From Acts ii. 46, we learn that a Daily Breaking of this Bread seems to have been customary with the Apostles and first Converts. And from Acts xx. 7, we conclude, that, even if a Daily Service were impossible, they all came together, at least, on the LORD's own Day, to celebrate the LORD's own Service. In those first days, full of danger and difficulty, in which also the first converts were mostly persons of such station in life as would prevent them from having much leisure, it is not unlikely that the Holy Eucharist was, for most of them, confined to the LORD's Day. Less than this, however, was never tolerated; the Sunday Service was never completed without the Celebration of these Holy Mysteries.

As soon as the Church became settled, the Daily Breaking of this Bread seems to have become a general custom for all devout members. And the Celebration every LORD's Day was so universally observed, that for the first three hundred years there is no trace of any custom to the contrary. It is, indeed, very remarkable that for the Public Worship of the Church for the first ages there was no Liturgy appointed, but only for the Holy Eucharist. No traces of any public Services have come down to us from the first three centuries, except the Liturgies belonging to the Eucharist.

So that it is an undoubted fact, that the practice of

the Primitive Church was constantly to celebrate the Holy Eucharist, at least, every LORD's Day.

To this Scriptural and Primitive practice we are most solemnly bound to return. Not to celebrate the LORD's own Service at least on every LORD's Day must be a most hurtful and grievous omission indeed.

Another consideration should here be added; that, as we cannot do even any *common* action, much less any *great* action, *well*, the *first* time we do it; as it is only by frequent practice that we can learn to do any great thing perfectly; even so it is with respect to our attendance at this our One infinitely Great Service. If we attend it only once or twice a year, we may be quite sure that we attend in a very poor and imperfect manner indeed. It is only by *frequent* attendance that we can learn how to attend *properly*.

The expressions in our own Prayer Book also cannot be satisfied without a weekly Celebration of this Holy Service; for it is there said to be ordained "*for the continual remembrance of the Sacrifice of the Death of Christ;*" and that it is instituted for "*a perpetual Memory of that His precious Death.*" Less than *once a week* surely cannot be called "*continual*" or "*perpetual.*"

Besides, a special Epistle and Gospel are expressly arranged for each Sunday and Holy Day; and this being for the Eucharistic Service only, it is plain that the Church intends us to have this Holy Service at least on every Sunday and other Holy Day.

Whatever objection may be raised against such a frequency may be raised as well against the frequency of Prayer, and so the wisdom of the precept, "*Pray without ceasing,*" would be questioned.

If it be better to pray often than to pray seldom, it follows that the One great Act of Prayer Divinely appointed for us in this Holy Service should be very frequently used.

There remains one other consideration, of very

great importance. How often is this most Holy Communion necessary for the due life and growth of our souls in Heavenly Grace?

A very great frequency is necessary, we all know, in taking our natural food, for the repairing of our daily decays and exhaustions, and for maintaining the due growth, and strength, and vigour of our bodily life.

Why, then, are so many of us in a state of such extreme spiritual weakness and decay, so barren and unfruitful in the knowledge of our LORD, but from the dangerous infrequency of our reception of That which is Meat indeed and of That which is Drink indeed! Surely the daily decays and exhaustions of our Spiritual Life require very frequent supplies of That which is our true Spiritual Food and Sustenance. Ought we not daily to seek for our "*Daily Bread*" in its highest and truest sense?

Whether, therefore, we consider this Holy Ordinance as the one Divinely-appointed way for showing the LORD's Sacrifice, the One great Act of Worship for the Christian Church, or as the One Divinely-appointed way for obtaining our True Spiritual Food, we must surely conclude that a *weekly* Celebration of it, at the very least, is our most bounden duty and our most heavenly privilege. The omission of this weekly Service is surely a very great dishonouring of GOD's Holy Worship, and a very great loss and damage to our own souls.

THE CHRISTIAN ALTAR.

"*We have an Altar, whereof they have no right to eat which serve the Tabernacle; for the bodies of those beasts, whose blood is brought into the Sanctuary by the High Priest for sin, are buried without the camp.*" (Heb. xiii. 10, 11.)

The Apostle here makes an emphatic assertion, and then gives a reason for it. Both the *assertion* itself, and the peculiar *reason* given for it, require careful attention, before they can be rightly understood.

The *assertion* is that we Christians have an Altar, whereof they who serve the Tabernacle have no right to eat.

The *reason* why they who are under the Jewish Law have no right to partake of the Christian Altar is that it was strictly commanded by that Law that the bodies of those animals whose blood was carried into the Holy Place by the High Priest, to be there offered *for a Sin Offering*, should be wholly burnt by fire outside the camp.

It will be easier to consider *the reason* first. This is founded on the Law of Jewish Sacrifices. These Sacrifices were of various kinds and for various purposes; some for Burnt Offerings, some for Peace Offerings, and some for Sin Offerings.

It is only and expressly to *the Sin Offerings* that the Apostle here refers. And amongst all the Sin Offerings, the Apostle refers to those only in which it was ordered that the Blood should be carried into the Holy Place by the High Priest, and there offered for sin before GOD, as the Divinely-appointed means of making Atonement and Propitiation for sin.

In the case of *such* Sin Offerings, it was strictly forbidden that either the Priest or the Offerer should eat of the flesh of the Sacrificed animal. (Lev. vi. 30; xvi. 27.) In the case of *other* kinds of Sacrifice, it was not only lawful, but it was commanded, that the Priest and the Offerer should eat of the Sacrifice.[1]

In the case of the Peace Offerings, a Feast upon the Sacrifice was an essential part of the Institution; but for the Sin Offerings there was no such Feast upon the Sacrifice.

In the case of all those Sin Offerings, in which the Blood was offered before GOD in the Holy Place for an

---

[1] Of the Blood, however, it was strictly commanded that no one should ever eat, either of any Sacrifice, or of any animal whatever.

Atonement, the bodies of the slain animals were not to be eaten of, but they were to be wholly consumed by fire outside the camp.

Now *that* which all the Sacrifices of the Jewish Law signified and prefigured in type and prophecy, and most especially so these Sin Offerings, is the One only real Sacrifice, even the Sacrifice of the very Lamb of GOD Himself. In all particulars He fulfilled all the Jewish typical Ordinances, and especially so those typical Sacrifices which were offered for Atonement. In every particular He fulfilled the type of the Sin Offering in Heavenly truth and tremendous reality.

His sacred Body was offered in Atonement for sin, an infinite Sacrifice unto GOD: "*He suffered without the gate,*" He was cast forth beyond the walls of Jerusalem, like the Sin Offering of old, as an accursed thing laden with sin, consumed "*without the camp;*" and then He Himself, having risen from the dead, and ascending into Heaven, began to be our Great High Priest in the Presence of the FATHER; and He entered in within the vail, S. Paul writes, "*with His own Blood,*" to offer it before the true Mercy-Seat in the Sanctuary above, to present it continually as the true Atonement for sin; to be, not a transitory action, but a continual "*Propitiation for our sins,*" thus fulfilling the ancient Type.

Now the Blood of this Divine Victim being thus carried in by the High Priest Himself into the Holy of Holies, to be there offered for Atonement for sin before GOD, no one who was under the Jewish Law might eat of the Body of such a Sin Offering.

Nevertheless our LORD Himself has instituted a Holy Ordinance for the whole Christian Church, to be its most distinguishing Act of Worship and Means of Grace, in which He expressly commands us, saying, "*Take, eat; This is My Body.*" The Bread which we break in this Holy Eucharist, S. Paul therefore declares to be, "*the Communion* [or the Partaking] *of the Body of Christ.*"

In this respect, therefore, this Holy Ordinance of CHRIST is certainly *the Feast upon the Sacrifice*. We Christians are not forbidden to eat of this Sacrifice, although it is the great Sin Offering; but, on the contrary, we are commanded to eat of it.

Thus, then, for the instruction of the Hebrew Believers of that time, S. Paul here speaks of the unprofitableness of their former observances, and then tells them that, as Christians, they were admitted to a most singular privilege, a privilege which belongs only to the Sacrifice of the New Covenant; for now all Christians are allowed and commanded to partake of the Divine Sacrifice, even of the true Sin Offering, which thing by the Jewish Law was strictly forbidden.

The Holy Communion of the Body and Blood of CHRIST affords to us Christians a privilege which would be emphatically denied us, if we were living under the Jewish Law of Sacrifices.

Thus much, therefore, the Apostle's assertion seems most distinctly to affirm, that *we* Christians *have an Altar, from off which* we partake of the True Sacrifice.

The Jews, as such, had no right to partake of the Sacrifice from off this Christian Altar, inasmuch as this Sacrifice is the real Sin Offering, Whose Blood is now carried in and offered before the very Mercy-Seat of GOD by our Great High Priest Himself for Atonement and Propitiation for sin; because the Jewish Law strictly forbade a Jew to eat of a Sacrifice which was such a Sin Offering.

When, therefore, we carefully consider this passage of Holy Scripture, we cannot but conclude that it gives us express authority for calling *that structure* (whatever it may happen to be) from off which we "*eat the Flesh of Christ and drink His Blood,*" our *Christian Altar*.

The Altar of which S. Paul speaks is one *from off which* we Christians have permission and power to eat. It is an Altar of Holy Communion; and there is no other such appointed for us but only that of the Holy Eucharist. Standing at this Altar, S. Paul speaks to us and says expressly, "*This Bread is the Communion of the Body of Christ.*" Nay, more; at this Altar our Great High Priest Himself speaks, and says to us, "*Take, eat; This is My Body.*" It is the Altar of our most Holy Communion. It is the Altar *from off which*, in a holy Sacrament and mystery, we do verily and indeed take and receive the Body and Blood of CHRIST.

It confirms us in this conclusion very strongly indeed, when we consider that this passage of Holy Scripture was uniformly interpreted in this sense by all the early Church writers, and that the name *Altar* was the one commonly given by them to the LORD's Holy Table. S. Ignatius, for instance, (who was the disciple of S. John, Bishop of Antioch, and Martyr) uses the very same original word, which is translated *Altar* in the passage before us, in three of his Epistles, for the LORD's Holy Table. Surely this intimate friend and companion of the Apostles must have very well known their mind on this matter.

In the writings of the early Church the name *Table* is but seldom used, but the name *Altar* frequently. The learned Mr. Mede thinks that the name *Altar* was the one usually employed for the first two centuries, and that the name *Table* is not to be found in any author of those centuries whose writings are now extant.

We cannot, therefore, but conclude that it is agreeable to Holy Scripture, as understood by the Primitive Church, to call *that* from off which we partake of the LORD's most precious Body and Blood *our Christian Altar*.

We Christians *have an Altar*, therefore, far superior to all that were called Altars in the former ages. For on those ancient Altars they showed only the figure and type of the one true Sacrifice before GOD, and then from off those Altars they partook only of those typical Sacrifices. But we Christians have an Altar of far superior dignity; for on ours we offer and represent before GOD That of which it is said, not, "*This is a figure or type of My Body*," but, verily and indeed, "*This is My Body*," the true Sin-Offering; and then, from off our Altars we receive, not the flesh of bulls and of goats, but, verily and indeed, "*the Flesh of Christ*," in a most heavenly profound mystery: here we are made *partakers of the One True Sacrifice*.

Is not our Christian Altar, therefore, infinitely more worthy of the Name, than all that were before it? We have the very reality itself, they only had the figure; they had the type, we have the very Antitype.

It is, of course, most deeply to be lamented, that to please the ignorant prejudices of some foreign Reformers, the Church of England laid aside the use of this holy Name at the last revision of her Prayer Book. This was a very grave fault, very painfully separating us, by the disuse of this holy Name, from the language of the Primitive Church. We must, however, pray for a better day, when this Name may be restored to that Office to which it so undoubtedly belongs. In the meanwhile it is enough for us to know that the holy Name *Altar* is used in the New Testament, if it is not in our Prayer Book. [See Note C.]

THE SACRAMENT OF CHRISTIAN UNITY.

"*For we being many are One Bread and One Body; for we are all partakers of that One Bread.*" (1 Cor. x. 17.)

Can it be supposed for an instant that the Divine Head of the Church has not made all-sufficient provision for the Unity of His Church on earth? Has not He Who so often spoke of His Church on earth as a Kingdom, furnished that Kingdom with perfect Means and Bonds of Unity? Are all Kingdoms upon earth constituted in Unity, and *not* the Kingdom of CHRIST? Is *that* which S. Paul calls "*the Body of Christ*" not indeed organized in perfection of Unity?

If even Jerusalem of old was built in Unity, which was only a figure and type of what was coming, *how much more* must "*the City of the Living God*" be built in Unity, which is indeed the New Jerusalem, which is now "*the Mother of us all?*"

All men desire and seek for Unity; but GOD Alone can give us the effectual means of real and enduring Unity. Man built Babel, but GOD built Jerusalem; and Babel soon became the city of confusion and division. And so did Jerusalem also, some may say; yes, but through the sin of man, not from any defect in its Divinely-organized constitution; only through the sin of man, who kept not the means and the bonds of Unity which GOD had ordained.

So it is, again, perhaps we may say, in the very Church of CHRIST; Christian Unity seems everywhere broken to pieces and shattered: we seem to be living in Babylon, rather than in Jerusalem: but this is owing, not to the defective constitution of the Church, but to our disuse, or to our too little esteem, of those Means and Bonds of Unity which are ordained for us by CHRIST.

The Church of CHRIST was and is intended to be for the perfect Unity and Brotherhood of Mankind, both outwardly and inwardly; it is designed and constituted to be the Means of uniting all men in a New and Divine Unity; so that all the Disciples of the LORD JESUS may be "*perfectly joined together*," having "*no divisions*" among them. The Apostle says, "*no divisions;*" so that the last Prayer of our dying SAVIOUR may be perfectly fulfilled, "*that they all may be One, as Thou, Father, art in Me, and I in Thee; that they also may be One in Us; that the world may believe that Thou hast sent Me."* (S. John xvii. 21.)

For the constitution and for the preservation of this Unity, most surely, our LORD has given and ordained all the Means and Bonds which are necessary. The only duty left to us in the matter is, *to endeavour, with all earnestness, to keep that unity which is already thus established for us.*

The only way in which we may ever hope that Unity may be once more restored to the Church, is by our returning to those Means and Bonds of Unity which our LORD has ordained for us, *not* by our trying to invent new Means or new Bonds of Unity for ourselves, which are merely human efforts, which soon fail of their end and come to nothing.

Nothing, therefore, is of more urgent necessity, in the present day of religious division, than that we should consider with the utmost concern *what are* the Means and Bonds of Christian Unity which are Divinely given us.

These are enumerated in several places in the New Testament: for instance, of the primitive Believers it is written, that *" they continued steadfastly in the Apostles' Doctrine and Fellowship, and in breaking of Bread, and in Prayers."* (Acts ii. 42.) Here are *four* of the most fundamental Principles, and Means, and Bonds of Christian Unity; apart from which Christian Unity does not exist. Then S. Paul gives us *seven* most fundamental Principles and Bonds of Unity in these words: *" There is One Body, and One Spirit, even as ye are called in One Hope of your calling, One Lord, One Faith, One Baptism, One God and Father of all."* (Eph. iv. 4—6.) As it is also written in 1 Cor. xii. 13, *" By One Spirit are we all baptized into One Body."* And another elementary principle and bond of Christian Unity is Divinely given us in Heb. xiii. 17, which is this: *" Obey them that have the rule over you, for they watch for your souls;"* which is the Principle of Obedience to One spiritual Ruler.

Now, for our present purpose, it is sufficient that we should collect, out of these fundamental Principles of the Christian Religion, *that provision which is made for Unity of Public Worship in the Church of Christ.*

For *Unity of Public Worship* is the daily practical Fruit of all principles of Unity. To be disunited in Public Worship must ever be one of the most unhappy marks of the loss of Unity that can exist. Surely, if we had to begin all things afresh, if we wished to unite a People together, our very first concern would be to unite them together continually in Acts of Public Worship. This is taught us even by the principles of Natural Religion. We need no Revelation to convince us of the propriety and duty and advantage of Unity in Public Worship. What heathen Nation or Tribe is there upon the face of the earth which is not united together in its Acts of Public Worship? How much more should this Unity consist in perfection among Christians.

If we look back upon the Means and Bonds of Unity which GOD ordained for the Unity of His People of old, how very strongly marked do we see this Unity in Public Worship; what absolute Laws, repeated over and over again, were given for this very purpose: "*Take heed to thyself that thou offer not thy Burnt Offerings in every place that thou seest; but in the Place which the Lord shall choose in one of thy Tribes.*" (Deut. xii. 13.) And in the sixteenth chapter the same Law is repeated *five* times. So that the Psalmist, understanding this essential Means and Bond of Unity, writes, in the 122nd Psalm, "*Jerusalem is built as a City that is at Unity in itself: for thither the Tribes go up, even the Tribes of the Lord, to testify unto Israel, and to give thanks unto the Name of the Lord.*"

That, therefore, which even Natural Religion teaches, that which the constitution of the Jewish Church so eminently sanctioned and provided for, namely, *Unity in Public Worship*, the Christian Religion must surely lead us to fulfil in the most perfect Form possible.

What are the Means and Bonds, then, which are now Divinely ordained for us, for this end?

First of all, by One Baptism we are all baptized by One Spirit into One Body, even into the Mystical Body of CHRIST. Being baptized, we are "*the Body of Christ, and Members in particular*," i.e., *one by one*. (1 Cor. xii. 27.)

By this Holy Sacrament, therefore, ordained for this end by CHRIST Himself, the Divine Head of the Body, we are all formed into One Holy Brotherhood, One New Society, the New Jerusalem, "*the Church of the Living God.*"

Next, in this Holy Society or Communion there are "*the Ministers of God and the Stewards of the Mysteries of Christ*," duly appointed, *set over* the people *in the Lord*. And the Divine Precept is that we should all obey the Spiritual Ruler. (Heb. xiii. 17.)

And as we may say that the very highest Object of the formation of the Church of CHRIST is to call us together out of the world to worship GOD in the Name of the LORD JESUS CHRIST, it is plain that these two Principles alone are sufficient to keep us together in One New Body in the Unity of Common Worship. For if we presume to offer Worship to GOD apart from those fundamental Laws which GOD has laid upon us, we can have no manner of lawful assurance that He will accept such self-appointed Worship. (See the note at the end of this Chapter.)

But now we come to the special subject before us. The Divine Head of the Church has been pleased to ordain for us *One special Act of Worship*, to be the One distinguishing Act of Christian Worship, even till He come again.

The Holy Eucharist is the only Service appointed for us all by the Head of the Church. The Church

Universal is therefore infinitely bound to use this Divine Service continually; and to celebrate this in Unity must ever be one of the essential duties belonging to every one who is baptized into the Body of CHRIST.

This is the one Worship of the whole Church, and the only one which we are absolutely bound to use. The whole Church upon earth has therefore thus one Worship, one Ritual, and one Altar; all the Altars of Holy Communion throughout all the world being one before GOD, by reason of the Presence of Him Who is the true Priest at every Altar, Who is present at the very Heavenly Altar above, presenting there the prayers of all His Saints.

What if the first Disciples of the LORD JESUS had not worshipped Him in Unity of Public Worship! What if they had not been united in this central Act of Worship! And is it any the less shocking in our day, that it should not be so?

But the Holy Eucharist is not only the Centre of our Worship, in which we are all united in one with the Worship above; but it is also ordained to be the great actual means, in the hands of the HOLY GHOST, for the continual preservation of our union in the mystical Body of CHRIST, through the Divine Gifts therein communicated to us.

For consider now what S. Paul writes concerning the Holy Eucharist, as it is thus the Means and Bond of Christian Unity.

"*We, being many, are One Bread, and One Body; for we are all partakers of that One Bread:*" and the Apostle had just been speaking of "*the Bread which we break*" in the Holy Eucharist, and saying concerning it, "*The Bread which we break, is it not the Communion of the Body of Christ?*" (verse 16.)

Our Christian Oneness, the Apostle teaches us, essentially depends upon *our partaking of that One Bread which is the partaking of the Body of Christ.*

The original language would be more strictly rendered by the words, "*We, being many, are One Loaf;*" and so the truth to be conveyed would be more strikingly expressed to us. As in One Loaf there is a perfect Union of many individual grains of wheat, even so we, being many, are hereby One Body, being all made partakers hereby of the Body of CHRIST, and so united in mystical Unity one with another, and all with Him Who is our Life-giving Head. For it is one of the essential properties of a Head to unite all the Members in One Body.

And, again, as the juice of many grapes is here pressed out into One Cup, even so the Apostle would teach us from this very analogy, we, being many, are One Body, being all hereby made partakers of that One Cup which is the Holy Communion of the Blood of CHRIST.

It is indeed perfectly true, and ever to be confessed, that the One Living Centre of Life and Unity for the whole Church is essentially in the Person of our Incarnate LORD Himself. He is the Second Adam for our New Generation, the One New Head Who binds all in One Body. The Church is "*the Fulness of Him Who filleth all in all.*"

Nevertheless He has Himself been pleased to appoint and ordain for our use certain Means of Grace and Life, certain Instruments and Bonds of Union, certain Joints and Bands, for carrying on His own Work amongst us upon earth. He has not left His Church on earth without giving to it a certain visible organization and definite Means of Unity within itself.

The Holy Eucharist He has made to be to us the Centre of our Worship and the very Bond of Unity, both of visible and invisible Unity.

For this Holy Sacrament, which we are infinitely bound to keep "*in One Body,*" has, like the other Holy Sacrament, *two parts; one* for visible, the *other* for invisible Unity; *one* Part, which is visible and earthly, marking us all and connecting us all outwardly, the *other* Part, which is invisible and heavenly, connecting us all with Himself, Who is the Living and the Life-giving Head of the One Body.

We, being many Members, are One Body, S. Paul teaches us, because we are all partakers of One Bread, even of that broken Bread of the Eucharist which is the Communion of the Body of CHRIST, even the Partaking of CHRIST Himself.

Here, then, is the very Central Means and Bond of Unity, both visible and invisible, for the whole Church on earth. Until we learn to know and to believe this, all our efforts for the restoration of visible unity will fail of their end.

For this Holy Eucharist is the Divinely-ordained Sacrament of Unity, apart from which all pretended Unity is but the empty shell. Here is the point at which the seen and the unseen meet and touch and are united in mystical Union. Here GOD and Man are joined together; for here is the Link which binds us on to Him Who is the Living Centre of the Church's Life, and so to GOD the FATHER of all. Here is the Centre of our Worship on earth, the Centre of Christian Unity, where the lowest is joined on to the Highest; for by this Holy Communion we are all made One with CHRIST, and CHRIST with us. This alone is our real, true, and enduring Unity; this is a Divinely-constituted Unity.

Thus the Church of CHRIST, the New Jerusalem, is built *as a City that is at Unity in itself*. Every other city built for Unity by man instead of this One City of the Living GOD is nothing better than Babel. No human inventions can ever "*reach unto heaven;*" only a Divine Institution can ever connect us with GOD. Whatever efforts we make for Unity, in forgetfulness of the Bonds of Unity which CHRIST Himself has given us, are valueless and fruitless, being "*not according to knowledge,*" however zealous or well-meaning they may be; and we only make ourselves like the builders of Babel again, no better, no wiser;

our own centres of Unity soon turning to nothing but division and confusion.

It is almost unnecessary to state that this Use of the Holy Eucharist, *as the Sacrament of Unity*, has for a long time been nearly lost from among us; so that we have fallen into a state of most unhappy and grievous disunion. Christians, of all people in the world, are now everywhere disunited in their Acts of Public Worship.

Supreme regard for the Ordinances of CHRIST has been laid aside, and human inventions have been put into their place; and the fruit is, even in this our day, a perfect Babel. Every man is building his own Babel, seeking for a Unity which is not of GOD. Do we not seem to be living in Babylon, rather than in the very and true Jerusalem?

We have quite forgotten that the only visible Centre of Unity for us on earth is *the Altar of the Holy Eucharist*. Only cast one look at the Altar itself in many and many a Church, and that look will be enough to convince us at once that little indeed is the value set upon that Service which belongs to it, little indeed is the knowledge of the Parishioners concerning the Holy Sacrament of Unity.

Yet this is the one only Divinely-appointed Centre for us all to meet around, till the LORD come again. Here is the hiding of our Life with GOD in CHRIST. Here the LORD Himself meets us with His special Presence. Here we are all made one with Him. Here is given us the very Bond and Link of Unity ordained by CHRIST Himself. For here we, being many, are all partakers of One Bread, even of that One Bread of which it is written, that it is, verily and indeed, "*the Communion of the Body of Christ.*"

All other so-called Christian Unity, apart from this, is but a hollow and deceitful shell, only a transitory delusion; for we dare not put aside any part of GOD's Holy Truth, out of feelings of Charity falsely so called. The Truth alone can ever bring us back to real Unity.

They who separate themselves from the One Altar of the Parish, openly violate the unity which CHRIST ordains and enjoins. They who set up Altar against Altar, out of their own private judgment, most grievously sin against Christian Unity. They who do not eat of the One Bread have no lawful right to consider themselves Members of the One Body; and *that*, we must consider and remember, is ever to be reckoned as the One Bread which is consecrated and broken by One Spiritual Authority, namely, by the Authority of the One Bishop of the Diocese.

NOTE.—A popular Objection to this is often made, which is founded on a misapprehension of our LORD's Promise, " *Where two or three are gathered together, in My Name, there am I in the midst.*" This Promise, being misunderstood, is used by many in the present day as a means of completely destroying all Christian Unity in Public Worship.

For, as popularly understood, each little sect claims this special Promise of our LORD for its Assembly.

But the truth is that this Promise does really unite, not divide us in Common Worship. For we must not overlook *the condition* of the Promise, "*in My Name,*" i.e., with and by My Authority. Now how can an Assembly be called together *with the Authority of Christ*, when it is called together, not only *without*, but even contrary to the Authority of the Spiritual Ruler who is set over us in the LORD? If we neglect CHRIST'S own Ordinances, may we venture to believe that our Worship is acceptable? These unauthorized Assemblies, therefore, can in no wise claim to themselves this special Promise of our LORD's Presence, because *its condition* is perfectly disregarded.

THE EXTERNAL RITUAL.

This Holy Service and Sacrament, ordained for us by the Divine Head of the Church, is not simply an Act of Faith only, it is not simply an Act of our spirit only; it is not merely an Act of spiritual Worship: but it is essentially, by Divine Command, an external Act as well; it is suited to our double constitution of body and soul; it may be well compared to some excellent fruit in the kingdom of nature which has both an internal seed and an external coat or shell. And it is no mark of wisdom to despise the external shell in which the Creator has enclosed the precious seed.

This Holy Eucharist has for one of its Names in Holy Scripture "*the Breaking of Bread.*" Its Celebration must ever include this external Action, as well as also the external Action of *eating* of the broken Bread. These two external bodily actions are essential; the breaking of Bread and the eating of it, the pouring out of Wine and drinking of it.

This chief Service of the Christian Religion has therefore embodied in it by Divine Institution a twofold character: our LORD's Command is, not simply, "*This believe,*" or, "*This consider;*" but it is, "*This do.*" There is an outward action of the body to be done, just as well as an inward action of the soul. Our senses are to be used, as well as our faith.

And, moreover, the external bodily actions commanded to be done in this Holy Service are essentially and highly *symbolical* ones. They are not meaningless, but rather, most full of meaning. The breaking of the Bread, and the pouring out of the Wine, and then the eating and the drinking of these external materials of the earth, are essentially *symbolical* actions. The Holy Service is essentially the showing forth of the Bruising of the Great Redeemer; it is the representation of the Sacrifice of the SON of GOD; and it is also the sustenance and food of our very eternal Life by that which is Meat and Drink indeed; and all this is essentially symbolized, and shown, and meant by these external actions, these Divinely-ordained rites and ceremonies.

The one great Christian Service is thus made to be

a *symbolical* service by our LORD Himself. He Who ordained His own chief Services in the former Jewish Dispensation of His Grace, and made them all to be full of type and symbol, still, we see, continues the same principle, and institutes the chief Service for the Christian Dispensation in such a manner as to be not merely a spiritual Act, but an external one also, the external part of it being essentially symbolical.

Our LORD Himself, therefore, most expressly teaches and authorizes us to use symbolism still, even in our very highest Act of Worship.

And so, of course, it follows at once that symbolism, being thus made essential to the very heart of this Divine Service by the very Author of all Glory and Beauty and Symmetry and Harmony, it follows of necessity that authority is given to the Church to use also any other symbolism which may be judged meet, and fit, and needful for the celebration of all parts of this Great Service with becoming external dignity and honour.

For the Order and Manner of the external performance of the Service is left to be settled by the Church. And this necessarily involves some ceremony, some ritual, some bodily action, more than that which is thought of at first: for instance, as to the manner of breaking the Bread, and of pouring out of the Wine. For most surely, *every single point* in so Divine a Service ought to be duly cared for and arranged, out of that supreme reverence towards Him Who has left this holy Service in our keeping.

In any Act of Public Worship offered to the Majesty of Heaven, even natural religion suggests at once that great reverence and propriety of ritual ought to be used.

When we only think or talk about our Queen in our private houses, we should do so with becoming respect to her high position; for as we are commanded to " *honour all men,*" so especially is it added, " *honour the King.*" Much more respect and honour, however, must we show towards her, if she holds a Public Court, and we attend it on purpose to show our loyalty; on such a public occasion, our dress and our whole outward behaviour would naturally be expressive of our inward feelings.

How much more so must supreme honour and reverence be shown in every possible way, when we present ourselves at a Public Assembly of the Church before the special Presence of Him Who is our LORD and our GOD, Whom we must worship and glorify both with our body and with our spirit, which are GOD'S. (1 Cor. vi. 20; Heb. xii. 28, 29.)

In *that* therefore which is the one distinctive Act of Christian Worship, we are most surely bound to use the greatest possible reverence. For this, above all other Acts of Worship, the greatest degree of external honour is justly due. It ought to be distinguished above all other Services by proper marks of distinction.

A barn is enough, prayers made at the moment are enough, a ragged garment is enough, a pewter cup is enough, if such things are really *of our best*.

But here in England, considering the rental even of the smallest parish, are such things *of our best?* Suppose we give *thirty* shillings for our own table-cover, and only *five* for that of the LORD'S Holy Table; or suppose we give *fifty* or *five hundred* guineas for our own dinner plate, and only *five* or *ten* for that belonging to the Altar of GOD, are such things enough? Are the principles even of natural religion satisfied with such things? What does common instinct teach even heathen tribes to do? In their chief Acts of Worship, what costliness do we see, what marks of distinction and signs of sacred office are ever used!

And then if we consult Divine Revelation, when it once pleased GOD to institute His own modes of worship, and to ordain Rites and Ceremonies for His peculiar nation, what exact care was to be given to each minute particular; in what beauty and glory was the Temple itself and the officiating Ministers therein to be clothed; the vestments for the chief Services being especially ordered "*for beauty and for glory.*"

Are all the numerous chapters in the Old Testament, which describe all these Rites and Ceremonies, all these materials and instruments of Divine Service, no longer of any use at all? Are they not parts of that Holy Scripture, concerning which it is expressly written, that "*All Scripture is given by Inspiration of God, and is profitable for doctrine,*" &c.?

Surely this large portion of GOD's Holy Word is not written without some purpose, surely it is "*profitable*" to us in some respect.

The least then we can learn from it, is this never changing principle; that the Public Worship of GOD requires our best care in every particular; for His Honour in this world is very much concerned in all things that belong to His Public Worship.

This is the essential Principle, taught by natural instinct, and sanctioned by Divine Revelation, that we cannot take too much care to make every particular belonging to the Public Worship of GOD such as it ought to be in every possible respect.

Let us take one especial instance, namely, the garment to be used by the officiating Minister in Public Worship.

Our natural religious instinct prompts us to say, "Cover me with some official garment, when I appear before the congregation to minister unto GOD and to speak in the stead of CHRIST." The individual person should not appear, but only his sacred office. It should be seen at once that he officiates by authority. His dress should be an official dress. The very heathen feel this and act upon it everywhere.

Next, what does Divine Revelation teach? It most unequivocally sanctions the natural instinct. A special vestment was expressly arranged and commanded for the High Priest when executing his office.

The shape, the colour, the wearing of every part of it, the changing of it, &c. all was minutely ordered. It was distinctly commanded, "*for glory and for beauty.*" (Exod. xxviii. 2.)

From this Divine Revelation we must certainly gather the unchangeable Principle, that it is, not only the instinct of natural Religion, but also the revealed Will of GOD, that in the Chief Acts of His Public Worship the officiating Minister should wear a special and a distinctly official garment. This is both for the honour of GOD's Holy Service, and as well for the profit of the worshippers. The individual person should be sunk and lost in the Officiating Priest. This Principle must surely be carried on from Mount Sinai to Mount Sion. There is nothing in the Christian Revelation to change it. We do not want to have it re-affirmed. If not distinctly abolished, it must remain of necessity.

Consider a moment an analogous case; take the parallel argument of Infant Baptism. In the Old Testament, we find that by express Divine Command little children were to be received into the Covenant with GOD at eight days old. At the Coming of CHRIST, the Rite of Circumcision was abolished, and the Sacrament of initiation into the New Covenant of Grace was instituted in its place. Infants were not mentioned in this Institution of Baptism; the same Will of GOD therefore remained, namely, that they could and should be received into His Church still.

So it is in the case before us. It is the Will of GOD, taught by nature and sanctioned by revelation, that the Minister of GOD should be clothed in a special Vestment for Acts of Public Worship, and therefore, above all, for the One distinctive Act of Worship instituted by CHRIST Himself for His whole Church.

There is nothing whatever in the Christian Revelation to alter or revoke this principle. It is of necessity carried on from Mount Sinai to Mount Sion, just as the Principle of Infant Church-membership is.

Besides, we ought to consider, most seriously, that all the Rites of the Jewish Law were so ordained of GOD as to be express types and significant representations upon earth of the very Worship of Heaven under the Priesthood of CHRIST Himself; and that therefore it follows of necessity that the spirit and essential meaning and principle of them is now in force and is the same for ever.

The practice of the English Church, it must be confessed, has been for a long time in a very degraded condition, the chief Service of the Christian Religion being greatly overlooked and neglected amongst us, no longer being the one prominent feature of our Worship, seldom celebrated, and even then without its proper marks of honour and distinction; the officiating Priest having on no other garment than that worn at all ordinary services, and worn even by the choir-men and boys; and the Service itself, instead of being alone, coming in at the end of other inferior services when all are tired.

The Altar of CHRIST is, in too many places, as poverty-stricken and mean as anything can well be; so that a heathen man coming into the church could by no means whatever believe that *there* is the one Divine Service of the Church of CHRIST.

A heathen man in old time indeed in coming into the Temple of the Living GOD would have seen and felt and confessed that "*out of Zion, the perfection of beauty, God hath shined.*" But now it would be said of Zion, in too many churches, if we cast one look upon the poor mean unmeaning Altar of GOD and upon all about it, that it is "*the perfection of ugliness.*" And some good people do not mind its being so, deceiving themselves by words about "*the simplicity of the Gospel.*" But what parishioner can thus be expected to believe that *there* is the only centre of Christian unity for the parish; and that *there* is the only Divinely-ordained centre of Worship upon earth for each parish, apart from which Worship, all other Acts of Worship are as much in vain as all Acts of Worship would have been in former dispensations *apart from worship by Sacrifice.*

Now that we have been restoring Architecture, Music, and Painting, and the frequency of Celebration, shall we not restore the proprieties of the Celebration itself? Surely it would be most inconsistent not to do so; it would be as meaningless as if we were only concerned for the beauty of the shell, and thought nothing of the value of the living kernel!

How is it possible to suppose for a moment that amidst all our past miserable neglect, the Holy Eucharist has been kept in its proper state?

Must we not distinguish between the written Law and our degraded practice?

Ought we not to restore the use of the distinctive Eucharistic Vestment so plainly ordered by the law of the Church, notwithstanding all the weak and ill-informed prejudices against it?

Even Dr. Adam Clarke, in his Commentary on Exodus xxviii. 2, regrets that "*the white surplice in the service of the Church is almost the only thing that remains of those ancient and becoming vestments which God commanded to be worn for glory and for beauty.*"

And on S. Matth. xxviii. 3, he says that the Angel "*was clothed in garments emblematic of the good tidings which he came to announce. It would have been inconsistent with the message he brought, had the Angel appeared in black robes, such as those preposterously wear who are themselves successors in the Ministry of a once suffering but now risen and highly exalted Saviour.*"

Without entering into any further details, which would be beyond the purpose of this book, it must surely be concluded, that the external Ritual of the Holy Eucharist demands our most reverent care; that it should be in all its main particulars symbolical; that the Altar and the Priest should be distinguished by peculiar marks of honour and office; that we should do all in our power to restore the LORD'S Service to its proper state of external honour and dignity; so that once again it may be said amongst us, "*Strength and Beauty are in His Sanctuary.*" For GOD "*hath made everything beautiful, in his time;*" and why should His own most Holy Worship be conducted in unmeaning ugliness and nakedness, stripped of all appropriate accompaniments?

NOTES.

NOTE A.

On S. John vi.

Dr. Waterland allows that our LORD's strong way of expressing Himself, in His discourse at Capernaum, and His emphatic repetition of the same thing in the same or different phrases, are alone sufficient to persuade us, that some very important mystery, some very significant lesson, must be contained in it.

And yet, after examining and rejecting some other interpretations of our LORD's meaning, this learned Author arrives only at this conclusion, saying, that the true meaning is this : " That all who shall finally share in the Death, Passion, and Atonement of CHRIST, are safe ; and all that have not a part therein are lost. All that are saved owe their salvation to the salutary passion of CHRIST; and their partaking thereof (which is feeding upon His Flesh and Blood) is their life. On the other hand, as many as are excluded from sharing therein, and therefore feed not upon the Atonement, have no life in them."

Thus this author makes the eating of the Body of CHRIST and drinking His Blood to mean, (as he writes,) "the partaking of CHRIST crucified, participating of the benefits of His Passion," "partaking of the Atonement made by His Death and Sufferings." He allows indeed that our LORD's language in this discourse *may be applied* to the Eucharist, but says that it does not of necessity refer to it; as the Eucharist is only "one way of participating of the Passion."

Thus Dr. Waterland explains away the great Mystery revealed to us in the words of our LORD's discourse at Capernaum, and turns the most extraordinary words, "*Except ye eat the Flesh of the Son of Man*" into, "*Except ye have faith in Me and in*

My Atoning Sacrifice." This is so far below the truth that it can scarcely commend itself to our acceptance. How dare we venture to say that to eat the Flesh of the SON of GOD only means to feed upon His Atonement by faith? Surely by so saying, we miss the whole mystery of that union with the Second Adam, the Incarnate LORD, which is afforded us by means of the Holy Communion of His Body and Blood.

NOTE B.

ON THE REAL PRESENCE.

The most unsatisfactory theory of Dr. Waterland concerning this Mystery of CHRIST is contained in such passages of his Review as these:

"The words, '*This is My Body*,' and, '*This is My Blood*,' cannot mean, that this bread and this wine are really and literally that Body in the same broken state as it hung upon the Cross, and that Blood which was spilled upon the ground 1700 years ago. Neither yet can they mean that this bread and wine are literally and properly our LORD's glorified Body, which is far distant from us as heaven." "It appears more reasonable and more proper to say, that the bread and the wine are the Body and Blood, viz., the natural Body and Blood, in just construction." "They are appointed instead of them." "The Elements are not literally what they are called, but they are interpretatively and in effect the same thing with what they stand for. Such appears to be the true account of the symbolical phrases of the Institution." "Our LORD's own Body and Blood symbolically offered." "It is all one symbolical Body in the Eucharist supplying the place of the natural." "The symbolical Body and Blood (bread and wine) are there present; the rest is present only in a figure."

With regard to these statements it must be first of all remarked, that the Doctor speaks of the *natural* Body of our LORD; as if it were to be assumed that the question is concerning the Presence of the *natural* Body, which it certainly is not.

And, next, his theory of substitution, or authoritative representation, or of symbolical presence, falls short of the absolute certainty and tremendous precision of the Divine Words, "*This is My Body*." By the Doctor's theory the empty shell is present, but the kernel is absent; we are still under figures and symbols; our LORD, in placing the Eucharist in the room of the Passover, only puts one figure and symbol in the room of another, saying, in real meaning, "*This is a symbol of My Body*."

One other passage of this Author's Review must here be noticed, that the reader may be able to judge still more decidedly of the complete inadequacy of his exposition of the nature of this great Mystery of CHRIST.

"CHRIST'S Body as crucified and Blood as spilled are no more; His Body glorified is as far distant as heaven and earth, and therefore not present in the Sacrament, or, if it were, could not properly be eaten, nor be of use, if it could, since "*the flesh profiteth nothing !*"

In this passage it is surely hardly too much to say that there are as many misconceptions and misstatements as there are sentences.

In the first sentence the hypothesis is, that it is *Christ's mere natural Body as hanging on the Cross*, whose Presence in the Sacrament we believe in and partake of. But no one in his senses surely ever dreamt of such a dreadful thing.

In the next sentence, which relates to our LORD's glorified Body, it is asserted that this Body is in Heaven, and therefore *cannot be present in the Sacrament*. But this is to venture to apply human reason to that which is above its reach, and to make a positive assertion about the Presence of the glorified Body of GOD the SON, which it is surely utterly beyond all human power to make, inasmuch as we know nothing whatever of the Laws of the Presence of any spiritual Body, much less of the Body of GOD.

The third sentence asserts that, if the glorified Body of CHRIST were present in the Sacrament, *it could not be eaten*. But this is simply to contradict the Divine Words, "*Take, eat; this is My Body:*" this is to stumble at the Mystery, because it has two sides; a visible and an invisible one, an earthly and a heavenly one.

The next sentence is still more strange—"*nor be of use, if it could:*" just as if to partake of the Living Body, the Quickening Flesh of CHRIST, Who is our Life, were of no use; or just as if our LORD had not spoken those words, "*And the Bread that I will give is My Flesh.*"

And the last sentence is equally painful, actually giving as the reason for the preceding statement, that "*the flesh profiteth nothing;*" which saying of our LORD's, certainly relating only to the gross conception of some Jews who then heard Him, who supposed that our LORD did really speak of His mere natural flesh, has no reference whatever to the glorified spiritual Body of the SON of GOD, concerning which the saying is infinitely true and real, "*My Flesh is Meat indeed,*" quickening with the Power of eternal Life our whole being.

Dr. Waterland's theory about "*symbolical feeding in the Eucharist*," seems to amount to the same thing as that propounded by the Author of "*the Unbloody Sacrifice*," who writes that "the Bread and the Wine are the authoritative representatives of CHRIST'S Body and Blood;" and again, "When we say we offer the Body and the Blood, we do not mean the substantial Body and Blood of CHRIST, much less His Divinity; but the Bread and the Wine substituted by the Divine WORD for His own Body and Blood." They are, he says again, "full representatives of CHRIST'S Body and Blood:" and again, he contends that the Bread and the Wine are CHRIST'S Body and Blood, "*in power and effect, not in substance.*"

All these Interpretations change the words of GOD our SAVIOUR, "*This is My Body,*" into "*This is not My Body, but only a representation, or symbol, or figure of it;*" and so the Mystery is gone.

Bishop Jeremy Taylor, in his Life of CHRIST, writes with more accuracy and truth: "It is hard to do so much violence to our sense as not to think it Bread; but it is more unsafe to do so much violence to our faith, as not to believe it to be CHRIST'S Body." "We believe both what we hear and what we see. He that believeth it to be Bread, and yet verily to be CHRIST'S Body, is only tied also by implication to believe GOD'S omnipotence, and that He Who affirmed it can also verify it."

And again: "When we say we believe CHRIST'S Body to be *really* in the Sacrament, do we mean *that Body, that Flesh*, which was born of the Virgin Mary, that was crucified, dead, and buried? I answer, I know none else that He had or hath; there is but one Body of CHRIST, natural, and glorified; but he that says that Body is glorified which was crucified, says it is the same Body, but not after the same manner: and so it is in the Sacrament."

Bishop Cosin also writes: "Our faith does not cause or make that Presence, but apprehends it as most truly and really effected by the Word of CHRIST. In this mystical eating, by the wonderful power of the HOLY GHOST, we do invisibly receive the Substance of CHRIST'S Body and Blood, as much as if we should eat and drink both visibly."

NOTE C.

ON THE WORD ALTAR.

Bishop Jolly well explains the proper difference to be made in the use of the names *Altar* and Table: "We call *that* upon which the Gifts to be presented to GOD are laid, sometimes the Holy Altar and sometimes the Holy Table. In respect of the

Sacrifice, Altar is the name; and for the Sacrament, the Feast upon the Sacrifice, it is called *Table*. And thus, in the words of the Prophet, Altar and Table are names of the same thing: 'The Altar of wood was three cubits high, and He said unto me, This is the Table that is before the LORD.' (Ezek. xli. 22.)" And Malachi writes: "The Table of the LORD is contemptible." And to the same effect Brevint explains: "The Holy Eucharist to men is a sacred Table, and to GOD it is an Altar."

www.ingramcontent.com/pod-product-compliance
Lightning Source LLC
Chambersburg PA
CBHW020302170426

43202CB00008B/461